First Published in 1979 by
Sampson Low, Berkshire House,
Queen Street, Maidenhead,
Berkshire SL6 1NF

SBN 562 00118 2

Designed by Peter Kenny Ltd., Ewell
Filmset by Tradespools Ltd., and Filmtype Services Ltd.
Printed by Waterlows (Dunstable) Ltd. •

AUDREY ELLIS

Party
MENUS

MENU PLANNERS

Sampson Low

Contents

	Cook's guide	*ten*
	Introduction	*eleven*
	Decorative table setting	*twelve*
	Introduction to menus	*fifteen*
Sherry party *Serves 8*	**Fino (pale dry) sherry and** **Cream (dark sweet) sherry** **Puff pastry twists** **Tangy prawn dip** **Curried cheese dip**	*sixteen*
St. Valentine's Day buffet *Serves 8*	**Egg salad sandwiches** **Spring daisy cake with** **Orange angel frosting** **Coconut macaroons** **Doonside Valentine cake**	*eighteen*
Easter dinner *Serves 8*	**Easter turkey with potato nests** **Baked egg custard with** **Rhubarb compôte** **Lemon meringue basket**	*twenty*
Easter tea party *Serves 12*	**Hot cross buns** **Duck biscuits** **Simnel cake** **Easter nest cake** **Easter bonnet cake**	*twenty two*
Harvest Festival party *Serves 20*	**Roast turkey with festival stuffing and garnish** **Herb-roasted corn cobs** **Baked potatoes with butter** **Harvest cheesecakes**	*twenty six*
Wedding buffet *Serves 50*	**Wedding cake (2 tier)** **Cream cheese and herb ribbon sandwiches** **Chicken liver pâté pinwheels** **Sardine diamonds** **Festive stuffed eggs** **Mushroom and ham quiche** **New potato and green pea salad** **Rice and pepper salad** **Chicken and pimiento aspic mould** **Creamy Dijon dip with** **Chicken fingers in batter**	*twenty eight*

6

                    Spring fruit salad
                    German wine cup

Christmas catering for a   *Christmas Eve*   *thirty four*
family party   **Gourmet's egg flip**
Serves 8-10   **Hors d'oeuvres speared on**
                                  cocktail sticks
                                  Spreads with savoury biscuits
                                  Unusual hot hors d'oeuvres

                                  Christmas dinner   *thirty five*
                                  Consommé starters
                                  Roast turkey with
                                  Original turkey stuffings
                                  Cranberry orange sauce
                                  Port wine jelly

                                  Christmas Day supper   *thirty five*
                                  Cold roast turkey slices
                                  Snow frosted ham
                                  Celery sticks stuffed with cream cheese
                                  Crispy rolls and butter

                                  The sweets of Christmas   *thirty six*
                                  Light Christmas pudding
                                  Marsala sauce
                                  Hot rum sauce
                                  Beat 'n bake Christmas cake
                                  Brandied mincemeat
                                  Plum cake with rum syrup
                                  Petits fours
                                  Swiss roll with mincemeat cream
                                  Glacé fruits

Family picnic party   **Sausage and apple pielets**   *forty four*
Serves 8   **Filled celery sticks**
                                  Spiced chicken drumsticks
                                  Fresh herb scones
                                  Assorted cold meats
                                  Frosty chocolate bananas

Elegant alfresco lunch   **Individual smoked salmon quiches**   *forty six*
Serves 8   **Avocado cream**
                                  Cervelat salad
                                  Pippin salad
                                  Smothered peaches

Big barbecue party   **Barbecue grilled sandwiches**   *forty eight*
Serves 12   **Jumbo beef burgers**
                                  Chilli barbecue sauce
                                  Cheesey frankfurters
                                  Mexicali salad
                                  Liver sausage whip
                                  Uncooked tomato chutney
                                  Honeyed fruit kebabs
                                  Sweet afterthoughts:
                                      Cart-wheel bananas
                                      Toasted coconut squares
                                      Melba sauce
                                      Mocha sauce

Simple sausage barbecue party *Serves 12*	**Sweet and sour sausages** **Caernarvon salad** **Cheesey jacket potatoes** **Sausages with barbecue sauce** **Indian-style corn on the cob** **Hot crusty rolls and butter**	*fifty two*
Summer buffet lunch *Serves 8*	**Creamed prawn vol-au-vents** **Poached salmon trout in aspic** **Cucumber salad** **Strawberry cream flans**	*fifty four*
Candlelight buffet supper *Serves 8*	**Cheddar mushroom caps** **Scalloped eggs** **Peanut dip with crackers, celery and carrot sticks** **Hawaiian pork cubes** **Oven-baked rice** **Quick tuna curry** **Chocolate Viennese torte** **Hazelnut cream gâteau** **Cardamom coffee**	*fifty six*
Party drinks for children	**Florida flip** **Grapefruit soda pop** **Family fruit cup** **Devon cup** **Cola fancy** **Chocolate challenger** **Grapefruit glory** **Peppermint twist** **Iced coffee** **Chocolate slim shake** **Orange marvel**	*sixty*
Children's tea party *Serves 8*	**Bow ties** **Rolled pineapple sandwiches** **Fruity orange baskets** **Mandarin wedges** **Banana candles**	*sixty two*
Pancake party *Serves 8*	**Crab and sweetcorn pancakes** **Sausage and cheese pancakes** **Cottage cheese pancakes**	*sixty four*
More about pancakes	**Baked layered pancakes** **Savoury pancakes** **Sweet pancakes** **American griddlecakes** **Cinnamon honey butter**	*sixty six*
French flan party *Serves 8*	**French onion and leek flan** **Prawn and bacon flans** **Mocha meringue flans** **Orange gingerbread fingers** **Café Napoléon**	*sixty eight*
Chinese party *Serves 6*	**Chinese-style rice soup** **Perfection pork with celery**	*seventy*

Buttered noodles
Chinese toffee apples

Fiesta party
Serves 8

Paella
Spanish rice and sausage salad
Sangria

seventy three

Curry party
Serves 8

Eggs in curry cream
Fruited lamb curry
Fluffy boiled rice
Canned lychees with vanilla ice cream

seventy four

Pasta party
Serves 6

Party pasta with mussels
Tuna tetrazzini
Green lasagne with beef
Italian baked peaches

seventy six

Time-saver pasta party
Serves 12

Turkey and noodle casserole
Pasta shells with bolognese sauce
Turkey and artichoke savoury
Bunches of white and black grapes

seventy eight

Pizza party
Serves 8

Tray pizza
Mediterranean deep pizza

eighty

Engagement party
Serves 8

Avocado cheese flan
Crunchy crisp dip with crackers
Sweetheart gâteau
Meringue gâteau
Marrons glacés

eighty two

Bread, soup and cheese party
Serves 8

Sandwich loaf
Cottage loaf
Pizzas with mozzarella
Winter vegetable minestra
Sausage and bean soup
Cheddar cheese platter with radishes

eighty six

Toasted cheese party
Serves 6

Anchovy rarebits
Double-crust cinnamon apple pie

eighty eight

Adding inspiration to fruit
Acknowledgments
Index

ninety
ninety two
ninety three

Cook's guide

In this book, quantities are given in Metric, Imperial and American measures. Where ingredients are differently described in the U.S.A., the alternative name is given in brackets. All menus are to serve the number indicated.

Spoon measures: In general, teaspoons and table-spoons make handy measures, although not always completely accurate. 3 teaspoons equal 1 tablespoon and 8 tablespoons equal about 150 ml/$\frac{1}{4}$ Imperial pint. (If you use a standard measuring spoon, it actually holds 17.7 ml.) The American tablespoon is slightly smaller (holding 14.2 ml) therefore occasionally an extra tablespoon is indicated in the American column of measures. All spoon measures are taken as being level.

Liquid measures: Quantities are given in millilitres, pints and American cup measures. The American pint contains only 16 fl oz compared with the Imperial pint which contains 20 fl oz, and the American measuring cup contains 8 fl oz.

Can sizes: Since there is no absolute conformity among manufacturers in their can sizes, the exact quantity required is indicated. If, for example, a 396 g/14 oz can of tomatoes is required, the nearest equivalent you can find on the shelves may be up to 50g/2 oz larger or smaller. Generally speaking, this does not affect the success of the recipe.

Oven temperature chart: Few ovens are accurately adjusted. If you are not satisfied with the results given by your oven, test the temperature range with an oven thermometer and set your dial accordingly.

Oven temperature chart

	°F	°C	Gas Mark
Very cool	225	110	$\frac{1}{4}$
	250	130	$\frac{1}{2}$
Cool	275	140	1
	300	150	2
Moderate	325	170	3
	350	180	4
Moderately hot	375	190	5
	400	200	6
Hot	425	220	7
	450	230	8
Very hot	475	240	9

Party MENUS

Introduction

Food can make all the difference to the success of your parties. An elaborate menu which is lacking in imagination may not please your guests as much as something far simpler which is rather unusual. Exciting ideas for party fare abound in this book to inspire you.

Make a list of all your requirements beforehand because some items may need ordering in advance, like a big batch of French bread, or can be made and stored in your refrigerator or freezer. This very much reduces the burden of preparation on the great day and you are more likely to have plenty of energy to enjoy the party yourself.

Somehow it is always rather difficult to estimate exactly how much food is needed for large numbers because appetites vary. If you wish to provide amply, and most wise hostesses want to make sure they will not run out of food, choose one or two items which could be used up afterwards if they are not needed. It is better to have a second cream decorated gâteau in reserve rather than a huge surplus of fruit salad.

Many of the party menus given are for as few as eight people because this is an easy number to double up. The question of drinks to go with the food is left largely to your own discretion. Sometimes there is an obvious choice, such as tea. Lager is much nicer with curry than wine and jasmine tea would be ideal with the Chinese party menu. Italian wines are the perfect partners to both pasta and pizza parties. A sparkling white wine would be appropriate for the Engagement Party and Guinness for the Toasted cheese party. Cider is a festive drink and could not be bettered for a Harvest Festival supper, a barbecue or to take on picnics. Wine is a natural choice for all the other menus except of course for children who are well catered for in their own section.

Audrey Ellis

11

Party
MENUS

Decorative table settings

An attractively laid table increases the pleasure of eating and helps to enhance your reputation as a good cook and hostess. Each time you add to your stock of table linens, china, glass and so on, bear in mind the permutations you will be able to achieve. Generally speaking it is easier to 'mix and match', if you have one set of plain china and one patterned set. Chunky modern tableware does not mingle very happily with ornate classical designs but sometimes linen or natural wood backgrounds look equally well with both, particularly if you have a good supply of coloured napkins which pick up one shade in decorated tableware, or contrast strongly with a plain background colour. Candle and flower decorations should be used to harmonise the scheme but there are a few basic rules to remember.

1. A small over-crowded table with a large centrepiece is neither practical nor inviting to guests. A large table with a good deal of bare surface on display and a sparse little posy of flowers in the middle does not give a welcoming impression either. Always try to relate the size of the table, decorative touches such as flowers and candles, and the china.
2. The colour scheme is intended to enhance the food not compete with it. Certain very strong cold colours, such as blue or purple, do not set off the food to advantage and since eye appeal is just as important as taste appeal to most of us, take this into consideration.
3. However pretty some delicate pieces of tableware may look, if they are a problem to use they contribute nothing to the success of the meal. Glasses which tip over all too easily and cutlery with awkwardly shaped handles are poor investments. Consider the practical side before you buy any new tableware.
4. Plan your tablesettings so that guests need not waste time handing single items such as condiments round the table. For any party of more than four sitting down to a meal, it is helpful to have salt and pepper sets at both ends of the table and the same applies to small butter dishes. If the flower centrepiece has trailing ends, or tall slender candles are insecurely poised, check whether guests

might be in danger of catching and knocking over the whole towering edifice! Sit down at the table when the setting is completed and make sure that you and your guests will be able to see each other over the centrepiece.
5. Compose a menu that does not put undue strain on your stock of china and cutlery. Do not rely on having to hastily wash up a full set of tiny spoons or special forks in the middle of the meal for a later course.

Laying the table

Fortunately this is a task you can accomplish at your leisure before the guests arrive. Space out the chairs according to the number of your guests and try to ensure that no-one is badly placed, straddling a table-leg. If the table-top is exposed, give it a quick polish. Wipe or polish table mats, and if you are using a cloth, check that there are no fold marks, even if it means ironing the cloth after you have taken it from the linen cupboard. The same applies to napkins which may need a quick spray with starch and re-ironing, according to the way you intend to fold them. Get out all the pieces of china you will need and go through the menu at the same time to make sure nothing is forgotten. Have a soft dry cloth at the ready so that you can rub up any item which is not shining clean. Decide how many plates and dishes will be on the table at any one time and select the decorative features which may be fresh flowers, plants, a fruit bowl or a candle and flower arrangement. Go through the same drill with glasses and cutlery, not forgetting serving spoons and slices, and arrange the cheese board and coffee tray.

It is amazing how much confidence you have while you are cooking the meal if you know these rather fiddly and time-consuming tasks have all been taken care of.

A word about party food

Always write down the menu you have chosen to serve, not only because it helps you to set the table beforehand, but to consider the contrasts in colour, texture and flavour it includes. Even if you discover

you are planning a cream soup followed by chicken with rice, you can add interest by sprinkling your soup with finely chopped parsley or a shake of paprika pepper and then garnishing the chicken dish with lemon or orange wedges. At this point, however, it would be wise to change your mind about cauliflower as a vegetable and introduce carrots, Brussels sprouts or peas, with perhaps a really crisp salad instead of a second green vegetable. Following these two first courses, a crunchy meringue dessert would be preferable to a velvety fruit mousse.

Laying a formal table
The rules for placing cutlery and glasses are no longer extremely rigid, but generally speaking cutlery is laid at either side of the place setting in the order it will be used from the outside inwards. Sometimes a dessert fork and spoon are laid across the top and dishes such as a glass sundae dish standing on a saucer may be served with a teaspoon sitting in the saucer. A side plate is placed to the left of the setting, sometimes with a simply folded napkin laid on it. Glasses are placed at the top right of the setting, in the order they will be used, beginning close to the diner and moving towards the centre of the table. Each course should be placed in front of the guests ready served out, or the appropriate plates put in front of them by someone who then carries the dishes round and offers them to each person for self-service. The latter method is becoming less popular as there is rarely anyone available to help the hostess in this way. Decide before the party begins who will deal with the service of drinks, both aperitifs and at table, who will clear away dishes after each course, and who will be responsible for the food being ready and piping hot, or cold as the case may be, when required.

Arranging an informal buffet
If the room is large enough to give a choice, you must decide whether to place the table against a wall, or in the centre of the room so that guests can circulate round it. In a small dining room, the former choice is probably the only possible one but it does mean that there may be a traffic jam of guests at the table as those who serve themselves will not readily move away. Try to organise the setting so that guests move in at one end, collect plate, pass along the table selecting goodies as they go and take cutlery and napkin at the other end. It helps to keep circulation moving if drinks are served somewhere else from a separate table or makeshift bar. Food which can be eaten with the fingers or with a fork only would be best. Consider how your guests can manage plate, glass, napkin and cutlery if there is no table at which they can sit down. If the numbers invited exceed the resources of your china cabinet, choose a service and buy good disposable plates, etc. to match. At least it will ease the washing-up problem.

Napkin folding
Modern napkins are not nearly as large as those massive affairs made of double damask which our parents cherished. Therefore, it is not possible to make some of the classic folded shapes. However here are a few very effective ways to fold smaller napkins which add a pretty touch to your table.
1. Fold the napkin in four to make a smaller square and then coil one corner round to make a cone with a join underneath. Place it in a water glass with a roll inside.
2. Fold the napkin in half from corner to corner to make a triangle. Place cutlery along the fold and bring the points opposite the fold over the cutlery tucking it firmly underneath.
3. Fold the napkin in half from corner to corner to make a triangle. Bring the opposite points up to the fold and tie the folded napkin into a single knot.
4. Fold in two opposite points of the napkin to the centre and then fold in these sides again twice. Double the folded napkin in half and push the fold down into a glass.
5. Fold the napkin in half and roll up like a Swiss roll (jelly roll). Tie with a ribbon bow.
The old idea of using napkin rings has recently been revived. To make them part of your decorative scheme if you are using flowers, the top of each ring can be adorned with a tiny posy.

14

Party
MENUS

These party plans range from small informal gatherings for fun with your friends to an impressive wedding reception for fifty people. All the recipes are simple enough for you to cook at home although for big parties it is a great advantage to prepare ahead and build up your stocks of food in the freezer. Even a two-tier wedding cake can be made and iced in your own kitchen and in these days when professional catering costs so much, party food you can provide yourself is bound to cost far less. With the expertise this book gives you it should be even more delicious to eat. Choose one of the simple informal menus like the Fiesta or the Time-saver pasta party and you may well be inspired to cater on a grander scale in the future.

Sherry party Serves 8

**Fino (pale dry) sherry and
Cream (dark sweet) sherry
Puff pastry twists
Tangy prawn dip
Curried cheese dip**

Puff pastry twists

INGREDIENTS	METRIC	IMP.	U.S.
Puff pastry [paste]	225 g	8 oz	½ lb
Canned anchovies	50 g	2 oz	2 oz
Grated Parmesan cheese	25 g	1 oz	3 tbspn
Beaten egg			

Roll out the pastry thinly to two rectangles each 12.5 cm/5 inches by 20 cm/8 inches. Drain the anchovies on kitchen paper then pound until they are a smooth paste. Mix with the cheese and spread thinly on one piece of pastry. Top with the other piece of pastry and cut into strips each 2.5 cm/1 inch by 6.5 cm/2½ inches. Twist each strip and place well apart on a greased baking sheet. Brush with the egg and bake in a hot oven (425°F, 220°C, Gas Mark 7) for about 12 minutes, until golden brown and well puffed up. Makes 16.

Tangy prawn dip

INGREDIENTS	METRIC	IMP.	U.S.
Peeled prawns [large shrimp]	50 g	2 oz	⅓ cup
2 tbspn tomato purée [paste]			
Few drops Tabasco			
Mayonnaise	250 ml	8 fl oz	1 cup
Salt and pepper			

Pound the prawns to a fine paste. Beat the tomato purée and Tabasco into the mayonnaise and add extra seasoning if necessary. Beat in the pounded prawns. Pour into a small serving bowl and chill well. Serve with crudités and more prawns as dippers.

Curried cheese dip

INGREDIENTS	METRIC	IMP.	U.S.
Cream cheese	225 g	8 oz	½ lb
2 tbspn single cream [half & half]			
2 tspn curry powder			
1 tspn creamed grated horseradish			
2 tbspn lemon juice			
Salt			
Sprig of parsley			

Cream the cheese and gradually beat in the cream, curry powder, horseradish and lemon juice with salt to taste. When the mixture is smooth and well blended, pile up in a small serving dish and chill well. Garnish with the parsley sprig and serve with crudités.

St. Valentine's Day buffet Serves 8

Egg salad sandwiches
Spring daisy cake with
Orange angel frosting

Coconut macaroons
Doonside Valentine cake

Spring daisy cake

INGREDIENTS	METRIC	IMP.	U.S.
Fine plain [cake] flour	100 g	4 oz	1 cup
Castor [granulated] sugar	275 g	10 oz	1¼ cups
¼ tspn salt			
Egg whites	300 ml	½ pint	1¼ cups
1 tspn cream of tartar			
½ tspn almond essence [extract]			
1 tspn vanilla essence [extract]			

Sieve the flour with 2 oz/50 g of the sugar and the salt. Whisk the egg whites until they just hold their shape, then add the cream of tartar and the remaining sugar, one tablespoon at a time. Continue to whisk until soft peaks form. Add the vanilla and almond essences. Gently fold the sieved flour mixture into the meringue. Turn into an ungreased 10 inch/25 cm ring cake tin. Bake in a moderate oven (350°F, 180°C, Gas Mark 4) for 35 to 40 minutes or until the top of the cake springs back slightly when touched. Invert the cake tin and allow to cool completely before removing from the tin. Ice and decorate with marshmallow daisies and leaves.

Orange angel frosting

INGREDIENTS	METRIC	IMP.	U.S.
2 egg whites			
Castor [granulated] sugar	350 g	12 oz	1½ cups
Orange juice	65 ml	2½ fl oz	⅓ cup —
¼ tspn grated orange rind			

Place all the ingredients in a basin and place over boiling water. Whisk for 7 minutes or until the frosting will stand in peaks. Spread over the sides and top of the daisy cake.

Coconut macaroons

INGREDIENTS	METRIC	IMP.	U.S.
2 egg whites			
Castor [granulated] sugar	225 g	8 oz	1 cup
2 tbspn cornflour [cornstarch]			
Desiccated [shredded] coconut	175 g	6 oz	2 cups
1 tspn vanilla essence [extract]			

Place the egg whites in a bowl and whisk until frothy. Place the bowl over boiling water and gradually whisk in the sugar and cornflour. Continue to whisk over boiling water until the meringue begins to thicken on the sides of the bowl, about 2 minutes. Remove from the heat and stir in the coconut and vanilla essence. Drop teaspoons of the mixture on an ungreased baking tray lined with siliconised parchment. Bake in a cool oven (300°F, 150°C, Gas Mark 2) for 25 minutes, or until lightly browned and set.

Marshmallow daisies and leaves For each marshmallow daisy, dip scissors in water and cut across the flat side of a marshmallow to form petals. Each marshmallow makes 4 petals. Arrange 5 petals on greaseproof paper in a flower design, slightly overlapping petals. Colour some sugar yellow and some green with food colourings. Dip the inside of each daisy into yellow coloured sugar to coat the cut sides of the petals. Place a small piece of marshmallow in the centre. For leaves, dip a single petal in green coloured sugar. Arrange the daisies and leaves around the frosted angel cake.

Doonside Valentine cake

INGREDIENTS	METRIC	IMP.	U.S.
Shortcrust pastry mix [basic pie dough]	225 g	8 oz	½ lb
Cooking [baking] apples	450 g	1 lb	1 lb
1 tbspn water			
Soft [light] brown sugar	25-50 g	1-2 oz	2-4 tbspn
Grated rind of ½ lemon			
Butter	100 g	4 oz	½ cup
Castor [granulated] sugar	100 g	4 oz	½ cup
2 eggs			
Ground almonds	100 g	4 oz	1 cup
Plain [all-purpose] flour	25 g	1 oz	¼ cup
Few drops almond essence [extract]			
Little castor [granulated] sugar			

Make up the pastry mix according to the instructions. Roll out and use to line a 'heart-shaped' sandwich tin, or an 8-9 inch/20-22 cm round sandwich tin. Reserve pastry trimmings for lattice strips. Peel, core and slice the apples. Place in a saucepan with the water, brown sugar and lemon rind. Cook gently until the apples are soft. Beat well with a wooden spoon and allow to cool. Put butter and sugar into a basin, and cream well together. Beat in the eggs. Add the almonds, flour and almond essence and mix well together. Spread the apple purée over the pastry base. Spread the almond mixture over the apple. Roll out the pastry trimmings and cut into strips. Place strips in a lattice pattern over the almond sponge. Bake in a moderate oven (350°F, 180°C, Gas Mark 4) for 30-40 minutes. Sprinkle with castor sugar before serving. This cake is best kept for a few days in an airtight tin.

Easter dinner Serves 8

Easter turkey with potato nests
Baked egg custard with
Rhubarb compôte
Lemon meringue basket

Easter turkey with potato nests

INGREDIENTS	METRIC	IMP.	U.S.
Frozen turkey, defrosted	2½-3 kg	5-6 lb	5-6 lb
Melted butter	50 g	2 oz	¼ cup
Salt and black pepper			
STUFFING			
Streaky [Canadian] bacon slices	50 g	2 oz	2 oz
1 small onion			
2 stalks celery			
Butter	50 g	2 oz	¼ cup
Soft white breadcrumbs	50 g	2 oz	1 cup
1 tspn dried rosemary			
2 tspn chopped parsley			
Juice and finely grated rind of ½ lemon			
1 beaten egg			
POTATO NESTS			
1 egg			
1 tspn ground nutmeg			
Mashed potato	1 kg	2 lb	2 lb
Melted butter	25 g	1 oz	2 tbspn
Frozen sweetcorn kernels	225 g	8 oz	½ lb
Parsley sprigs to garnish			

Wash the turkey, remove the giblets and use these to make gravy. Cover the bird with melted butter and sprinkle with salt and pepper. To make the stuffing, chop the bacon, finely chop the onion and celery. Melt the butter and use to fry the bacon and onion until soft. Add all the remaining stuffing ingredients and seasoning to taste and leave to cool. Use to stuff the turkey breast. Place the stuffed turkey in a roasting tin and bake in a moderate oven (325°F, 170°C, Gas Mark 3) for 2¼-2½ hours. Baste the turkey every 30 minutes and cover with foil if necessary to prevent over-browning. To make the potato nests, beat the egg, nutmeg and seasoning to taste into the mashed potato and place in a large piping bag fitted with a rose nozzle. Pipe nests of potato on a well-greased baking sheet and sprinkle with melted butter. Place in the oven with the turkey for the last 30 minutes of cooking time, until golden brown on the edges. Meanwhile, cook the sweetcorn, drain and spoon into the nests. Garnish with parsley sprigs. Serve the turkey surrounded by potato nests and with a selection of spring vegetables and well-flavoured giblet gravy.

Baked egg custard

INGREDIENTS	METRIC	IMP.	U.S.
Milk	900 ml	1½ pints	3¾ cups
6 whole eggs			
Castor [granulated] sugar	50 g	2 oz	¼ cup

Place the milk in a pan and bring it almost to the boil, then remove from the heat. Break the eggs into a bowl and whisk lightly to blend with the sugar. Stirring all the time, pour on the heated milk. Strain and allow to cool. Pour into an ovenproof dish. Bake in a moderate oven (350°F, 180°C, Gas Mark 4) in a bain marie or a roasting tin, half filled with water, for 45 minutes or until custard is set.

Lemon meringue basket

INGREDIENTS	METRIC	IMP.	U.S.
2 egg whites			
Castor [granulated] sugar	100 g	4 oz	½ cup
Pinch salt			
4 tbspn double [whipping] cream			
Lemon curd	225 g	8 oz	½ lb

Prepare a baking sheet by covering it with a sheet of non-stick siliconised parchment. With a pencil, lightly draw an 8 inch/20 cm circle on it; (use a plate as a guide). Lightly brush with oil. Whisk the egg whites in a bowl until they are stiff. (If using frozen ones, defrost fully first.) Sprinkle in half the sugar and whisk until the mixture is as stiff as before. Using a metal tablespoon, gently fold in the remaining sugar with the salt. Spread half the meringue mixture over the marked circle, keeping within the pencilled outline. Put the remaining mixture in a piping bag fitted with an open star tube and pipe 16 rosettes round the edge of the meringue circle. Place in a very cool oven (225°F, 110°C, Gas Mark ¼) for 2-2½ hours, until completely dry. Remove from the oven, peel off the paper and cool the meringue case on a wire rack. Fold the lightly whipped cream into the lemon curd.

To serve the meringue, place it on a serving dish and spread the lemon filling in the centre.

Excellent freezables are uncooked egg custard and lemon curd. Make up the custard mixture and pour into a baking dish ready for the oven, or into small individual dishes lined with a caramel made by dissolving sugar in very little water and boiling until it is golden brown. For very special occasions make the custard mixture with cream instead of milk. Keep your home-made lemon curd in the freezer and just take it out a couple of hours before use; it will last all round the year.

Easter tea party

Hot cross buns
Duck biscuits
Simnel cake
Easter nest cake
Easter bonnet cake

Hot cross buns

INGREDIENTS	METRIC	IMP.	U.S.
Strong plain [all-purpose] flour	450 g	1 lb	4 cups
½ tspn salt			
2 tspn ground mixed spice			
Margarine	50 g	2 oz	¼ cup
Castor [granulated] sugar	50 g	2 oz	¼ cup
Sultanas [golden raisins]	50 g	2 oz	⅓ cup
Currants	25 g	1 oz	2 tbspn
Chopped mixed peel	25 g	1 oz	2 tbspn
1 egg			
About 6 tbspn milk			
Little marzipan [almond paste]			
YEAST LIQUID			
1 tspn sugar			
Warm water	150 ml	¼ pint	⅔ cup
2 tspn dried yeast			
GLAZE			
1 tbspn sugar			
1 tbspn milk			
1 tbspn water			

Sift the flour, salt and spice together into a bowl. Rub in the margarine. Stir in the sugar, dried fruit and peel. Prepare the yeast liquid. Dissolve the sugar in the water, sprinkle over the yeast and leave in a warm place for about 10 minutes until frothy. Beat the egg and add to the dry ingredients with the yeast liquid and milk. Mix well then turn out on a floured surface and knead well for about 10 minutes. Return the dough to the greased mixing bowl, cover and allow to stand in a warm place until double in size. Turn out and knead lightly. Divide into 12 equal portions and shape each into a round ball. Arrange on a greased baking sheet, cover and leave in a warm place until double in size. To make the crosses on the buns, either roll out the marzipan thinly, cut into strips, moisten and place on the buns, or cut a deep cross in the top of each bun with a sharp knife. Bake in a moderately hot oven (400°F, 200°C, Gas Mark 6) for about 15 minutes. Meanwhile, boil together the sugar, milk and water and use to brush the buns when they are removed from the oven.

Duck biscuits

INGREDIENTS	METRIC	IMP.	U.S.
Butter	115 g	4½ oz	½ cup +
Castor [granulated] sugar	100 g	4 oz	½ cup
1 egg			
2 drops vanilla essence [extract]			
Plain [all-purpose] flour	175 g	6 oz	1½ cups
Rolled oats [uncooked quick-cooking oats]	75 g	3 oz	1 cup −
Little apricot jam			

Cream the butter and sugar until light and fluffy. Beat in the egg and vanilla essence. Mix in the flour and oats to form a firm dough. Roll out on a floured board to a thickness of 0.5 cm/ ¼ inch. Cut into duck shapes with a fancy cutter and arrange on baking sheets lined with non-stick cooking parchment. Top with a little apricot jam and bake in a moderate oven (350°F, 180°C, Gas Mark 4) for 10-15 minutes, until firm to the touch and just pale golden. Cool on a wire rack.

Simnel cake

INGREDIENTS	METRIC	IMP.	U.S.
Self-raising flour [all-purpose flour + 2 tspn baking powder]	225 g	8 oz	2 cups
1 tspn ground mixed spice			
1 tspn ground cinnamon			
1 tspn ground nutmeg			
Glacé [candied] cherries	50 g	2 oz	½ cup
2 eggs			
Butter	100 g	4 oz	½ cup
Castor [granulated] sugar	100 g	4 oz	½ cup
Mixed dried fruit	225 g	8 oz	1 cup
2 tbspn orange juice			
2 tbspn milk			
2 tbspn apricot jam			
Marzipan [almond paste]	350 g	12 oz	¾ lb
6 tbspn icing [confectioner's] sugar			
Plain [unsweetened] chocolate	25 g	1 oz	1 square

Line a 17.5 cm/7 inch cake tin with non-stick cooking parchment. Sift the flour with the spices. Chop the cherries and beat the eggs. Cream the butter and sugar until light and fluffy. Gradually add the egg, beating well after each addition. Fold in the flour mixture and add the dried fruit and cherries, orange juice and milk. Turn into the prepared tin and smooth the top. Bake in a moderate oven (350°F, 180°C, Gas Mark 4) for about 1¼ hours, until a fine skewer inserted in the centre comes out clean. Cool on a wire rack. Cut the cake in half. Heat the jam with 1 tablespoon water then sieve. Use a little to brush the cut surfaces of the cake. Divide the marzipan in half and roll each portion to a 17.5 cm/7 inch round. Place one round between the two portions of cake. Brush the cake all over with the apricot glaze. Cut out the centre of the second round of marzipan. Place the circle of marzipan on top of the cake. Mould the remaining marzipan into 11 'egg-shaped' balls and arrange round the top edge of the cake. Add just sufficient water to the icing sugar to make a stiff paste and spread in the centre of the circle of marzipan. When this is firm, melt the chocolate, place in a small icing syringe and pipe the word 'Easter' in the centre of the cake.

Easter nest cake

INGREDIENTS	METRIC	IMP.	U.S.
Water	225 ml	7½ fl oz	1 cup −
Butter	75 g	3 oz	⅓ cup
Plain [all-purpose] flour	90 g	3¾ oz	1 cup −
Pinch salt			
3 eggs			
4 tbspn sieved apricot jam			
FILLING			
Canned apricot halves	425 g	15 oz	15 oz
Cream cheese	225 g	8 oz	½ lb
Double [whipping] cream	150 ml	¼ pint	½ cup
4 tbspn castor [granulated] sugar			
Ground cinnamon			
Pretzels			

Heat the water with the butter and bring to a fast boil. Sift the flour with the salt and add to the pan all at once. Beat until the mixture leaves the sides of the pan clean. Cool slightly then beat in the eggs, one at a time. Cool. Spoon half the mixture into a piping bag and pipe into a round measuring 17.5 cm/7 inches in diameter on a baking sheet lined with non-stick cooking parchment. Place the remaining pastry in the bag and pipe 18 small balls on another baking sheet lined with parchment. Moisten the parchment round the large base and bake altogether in a moderately hot oven (400°F, 200°C, Gas Mark 6). The base will take 20-25 minutes and the balls about 10 minutes. The pastry should be golden brown and well risen. Pierce each ball with a sharp knife to allow the steam to escape. Cool on a wire rack. To make the filling, drain the apricots, reserving the syrup, and chop them. Cream the cheese and mix in the apricots. Use half this mixture to fill the pastry balls. Spread the remainder of the mixture on the pastry base. Arrange the filled balls round the edge of the base, sticking them in position with a little jam if necessary. Whip the cream with the sugar and 4 tablespoons apricot syrup. Spread over the apricot mixture on the base of the cake and sprinkle with cinnamon. Arrange pretzels over the top. Heat jam with 1 tablespoon water, then glaze pastry balls.

Easter bonnet cake

INGREDIENTS	METRIC	IMP.	U.S.
All-Bran	50 g	2 oz	⅔ cup
Milk	150 ml	¼ pint	½ cup
Butter	140 g	4½ oz	½ cup +
Soft [light] brown sugar	100 g	4 oz	½ cup
2 eggs, beaten			
Self-raising flour [all-purpose flour + 1 tspn baking powder]	100 g	4 oz	1 cup
2 tbspn milk			
Sifted icing [confectioner's] sugar	50 g	2 oz	½ cup
1 tbspn water			
TOPPING			
Butter	15 g	½ oz	1 tbspn
1 tbspn golden [corn] syrup			
Corn flakes	25 g	1 oz	1 cup

Put the All-Bran and milk into a basin and leave to soak until the milk is absorbed. Cream the butter and brown sugar until light and fluffy, then gradually beat in the eggs. Add the All-Bran and flour and fold in. Mix to a soft consistency with the milk. Spread mixture in a greased and base-lined 8 inch/20 cm cake tin and bake in a moderate oven (350°F, 180°C, Gas Mark 4) for about 40 minutes. Cool on a wire rack. Mix the icing sugar and water together and spread over the top of the cake. To make the topping, place the butter and golden syrup in a pan and heat gently until the butter has melted. Remove from the heat and add the corn flakes. Stir until the flakes are coated with the syrup mixture. Spread over the top of the cake. Place cake on a doiley that is bigger than the cake, to represent the bonnet 'brim'. Place on a cake board. Tie a ribbon round the side of the cake in a bow.

Harvest Festival party
Serves 20

Roast turkey with festival stuffing and garnish
Herb-roasted corn cobs
Baked potatoes with butter
Harvest cheesecakes

Turkey tips For 20 people you will need a turkey weighing about 15 lb/7 kg. A bird of this size will need 5–6 hours cooking at 325°F, 170°C, Gas Mark 3. A big turkey takes time to cook but you can save yourself the trouble of frequent basting and anxiety about tenderness of the meat in any one of the following ways. Cook the bird in a large-size poultry roasting bag. This obviates the need to baste and keeps the flesh very moist and succulent. Or, coat the skin with a thin film of oil and put the bird in a roasting tin. Cover with extra-wide foil and crimp tightly under the edges of the tin. Easiest of all, choose a deep-basted turkey which already has fat inserted under the skin and virtually looks after itself. Just follow the instructions on the pack and you will be sure to have a tender bird with a crisp brown skin.

Festival stuffing and garnish Cook 2 tablespoons each finely-chopped red pepper, green pepper and onion in a little butter until soft and combine with a breadcrumb and herb stuffing mix. Surround the cooked turkey with fried bacon dice, cooked red kidney beans and rice tinted yellow by adding saffron strands to the water used for cooking. Use sprigs of watercress to garnish.

Herb-roasted corn cobs

INGREDIENTS	METRIC	IMP.	U.S.
Butter	*275 g*	*10 oz*	*1¼ cups*
2½ tspn dried marjoram			
2½ tspn dried rosemary			
20 corn cobs			
40 outer cabbage leaves			

Beat the butter with the herbs. Remove the husks from the corn cobs. Spread the herbed butter on each corn cob. Place 20 cabbage leaves in a lightly greased shallow baking dish. Arrange the corn cobs on top of the cabbage leaves and cover them with the remaining cabbage leaves. Cover tightly with foil, sealing well, and bake in a hot oven (425°F, 220°C, Gas Mark 7) for 25–30 minutes. Discard cabbage leaves.

Harvest cheesecakes

INGREDIENTS	METRIC	IMP.	U.S.
BASE			
Crushed digestive biscuits [Graham crackers]	100 g	4 oz	1½ cups
Swiss breakfast cereal [muesli]	100 g	4 oz	1 cup
Soft margarine	175 g	6 oz	¾ cup
4 tbspn castor [granulated] sugar			
FILLING			
4 eggs			
'Philly' soft cheese	450 g	1 lb	1 lb
Natural [plain] yogurt	250 ml	8 fl oz	1 cup
4 tspn clear honey			
2 tbspn gelatine [gelatin]			
Water	150 ml	¼ pint	1 cup
Castor [granulated] sugar	100 g	4 oz	½ cup
TOPPING			
2 red eating apples			
4 tbspn clear honey			
Small bunch green grapes			
Walnut halves			

To make the bases, mix the biscuit crumbs and breakfast cereal together. Melt the margarine and sugar together, stir in the cereal mixture. Press this mixture into the bases of two greased 20 cm/8 inch loose-bottomed cake tins. Chill. Separate the eggs. Cream the 'Philly' until smooth, gradually adding the egg yolks, yogurt and honey. Dissolve the gelatine in the water in a basin over a pan of hot water. Cool then add to the yogurt mixture. Whisk the egg whites until stiff. Whisk in the sugar then fold into the yogurt mixture. Pour on to the prepared bases and chill until firm. Meanwhile, prepare the topping. Quarter the apples and remove the cores. Slice thinly and poach gently in the honey until slightly softened. Cool. Carefully remove the cake tins, leaving the cheesecakes on the metal bases. Decorate with grapes, nuts and apple. Glaze with any honey left from poaching the apple.

Wedding buffet

Serves 50

Wedding cake (2 tier)
Cream cheese and herb ribbon sandwiches
Chicken liver pâté pinwheels
Sardine diamonds
Festive stuffed eggs
Mushroom and ham quiche
New potato and green pea salad
Rice and pepper salad
Chicken and pimiento aspic mould
Creamy Dijon dip with
Chicken fingers in batter
Spring fruit salad
German wine cup

Chicken fingers in batter are available frozen in boxes and only require frying for a few minutes to make them crisp and golden brown. Drain well before serving.

28

Wedding cake (2 tier)

INGREDIENTS	METRIC	IMP.	U.S.
Currants	400 g	14 oz	2¾ cups
Sultanas [seedless white raisins]	400 g	14 oz	2¾ cups
Seedless raisins	275 g	10 oz	2 cups
4 eggs			
Soft [light] brown sugar	275 g	10 oz	1¼ cups
Corn oil	275 ml	9 fl oz	1 cup+
Plain [all-purpose] flour	450 g	1 lb	1 lb
2½ tspn baking powder			
pinch salt			
5 tbspn red wine or sherry			
Chopped candied peel	175 g	6 oz	1 cup
Chopped, blanched almonds	150 g	5 oz	1 cup
Chopped glacé [candied] cherries	150 g	5 oz	½ cup

Line two round cake tins, one 8 inch/20 cm and one 6 inch/15 cm with parchment. Clean and dry the currants, sultanas and raisins if necessary. Beat the eggs, sugar and corn oil together. Sieve the flour with the baking powder and salt and stir into the oil mixture. Add the wine and fold in the fruit, peel, almonds and cherries. Turn the mixture into the prepared tins and smooth the tops. Bake in a cool oven (300°F, 150°C, Gas Mark 2) for 3-3½ hours. Cool on a wire rack.

A wedding cake with fondant icing is far easier to decorate than one laboriously coated in layers of royal icing. The fondant is rolled out like pastry, lifted over the cake on the rolling pin, and moulded down the sides. A smooth, firm surface for decorating is ensured in one simple operation which takes only a few minutes.

Fondant icing

INGREDIENTS	METRIC	IMP.	U.S.
FOR THE 8 INCH/20 CM CAKE			
2 tbspn water			
4 tspn unflavoured gelatine [gelatin]			
Scant 4 tspn glycerine			
Liquid glucose	125 ml	4 fl oz	½ cup
Sifted icing [confectioner's] sugar	900 g	2 lb	2 lb
Cornflour [cornstarch]			
FOR THE 6 INCH/15 CM CAKE			
4½ tspn water			
1½ tspn gelatine [gelatin]			
Generous 2 tspn glycerine			
Liquid glucose	75 ml	2½ fl oz	¼ cup+
Sifted icing [confectioner's] sugar	575 g	1¼ lb	1¼ lb
Cornflour [cornstarch]			

Put the water and gelatine in a pan and stir constantly over gentle heat until the gelatine has dissolved completely. Remove from the heat, add the glycerine and liquid glucose and pour into a bowl. Gradually add the icing sugar to form a stiff paste. Sprinkle the work surface with cornflour and knead the paste until smooth. Roll out, using only just sufficient cornflour to prevent the paste from sticking, lift on the rolling pin and smooth over the cake. Trimmings can be used to make moulded decorations or bought decorations can be used. The cakes can be stored in the freezer in large rigid-based polythene containers, or, if mounted on silver boards, in polythene bags, for a short period. If kept longer, although the icing does not dry out when defrosted, a slight discolouration may appear through the icing.

Wedding buffet

When you are called upon to provide elegant food for a hungry horde of say fifty people, you may find it difficult to work out the necessary quantities. If the result staggers you in terms of cost and preparation time for the feast, take heart. This menu is modestly priced; and if you possess a freezer much of the work can be done ahead.

My menu for an outdoor wedding reception, fête, flower show, or tournament is planned to be prepared ahead and stored in the minimum freezer space.

If our weekend weather is true to form, you may well be crouching under a hedge in the pouring rain, bemoaning the choice of date. If you are lucky, the weather will be idyllic and all will be bliss and strawberries or fruit salad and cream.

It is assumed each guest will sample 2 cold savoury dishes and 2-3 hot chicken bites, a portion of salad, one of cake and one of fruit salad. The choice of other drinks is your own. A sparkling Rhine wine adds as much verve to the occasion as champagne but is kinder to the purse. Strawberries, if picked locally depending on where you live, might be served with whipped cream and castor sugar instead of the fruit salad.

Making the food manageable: So much good wine is spilled, food mashed underfoot, and tempers tried at parties – just because guests cannot manage to hold a plate with one hand and eat with knife and fork with the other. Food for a buffet should always be easy to pick up or eat with a fork, and salad greens torn up sufficiently small to be easily speared.

Setting out the tables: Trestle tables need to hide their legs modestly under crisp white tablecloths for this kind of party. Freshly laundered lightly starched sheets will do very well. Providing the expanse of tabletop is long enough and the back is concealed, this can be left uncovered and additional supplies can be hidden away under the table to be brought forward as required.

Resist strongly the temptation to set out the food hours in advance. I cannot over-emphasize that arranging the food on the table too soon makes nonsense of your care in preparing it, because it will not look or taste fresh. It is infinitely better to have two extra willing pairs of hands to put out the spread at the last moment.

Sandwiches can be lovely, providing they are kept moist and the fillings are generous. They can safely be made in advance, trimmed and wrapped in foil to make compact parcels for economy of space in the refrigerator or freezer.

Cream cheese and herb ribbon sandwiches: Slice a large white loaf and a large brown loaf thinly, lengthwise, and remove the crusts. Spread with softened butter and sandwich four slices together (white and brown alternately) with softened cream cheese seasoned and mixed with chopped fresh herbs to taste. Wrap with dividers between the blocks and freeze in a neat foil parcel. To serve, remove dividers, allow the blocks to thaw sufficiently to cut into thin slices; if liked, cut each slice in half again.

Chicken liver pâté pinwheels: Cut slices from a large brown loaf lengthwise, remove the crusts and spread the slices with softened butter. Spread with pâté and roll up like a Swiss roll. If liked, place pimiento-stuffed olives along one of the short edges before rolling. Wrap, pack and freeze. To serve, allow the rolls to thaw sufficiently to cut into thin, round slices and arrange on a dish.

Sardine diamonds: Use 2 large thinly sliced loaves, one white and one brown. Make rounds of sandwiches in the usual way with mashed sardines seasoned with lemon juice, salt and pepper to taste. Wrap, pack and freeze in a neat foil parcel. To serve, allow the sandwiches to defrost sufficiently to remove the crusts, then cut into diamonds.

Festive stuffed eggs: Hard-boil 50 large eggs. Cool under running water and shell. Slice the eggs in half lengthwise, scoop out the yolks and place in a large bowl, mash and beat in 4 oz/100 g/$\frac{1}{2}$ cup softened butter and $\frac{1}{4}$ pint/150 ml/generous $\frac{1}{2}$ cup mayonnaise. Divide the mixture equally into three portions. Flavour one portion with approximately 2 teaspoons

Right: Sardine diamonds, Chicken liver pâté pinwheels, Cream cheese and herb ribbon sandwiches.

Wedding buffet

curry powder and salt to taste. Flavour the second portion with 1 tablespoon tomato purée, 1 teaspoon paprika pepper and salt to taste. Flavour the remaining portion with 1 teaspoon anchovy essence and a little white pepper to taste. Place the first mixture in a piping bag fitted with a large star nozzle and pipe into about 30 egg halves. Top each with a few capers. Add the second mixture to the bag and pipe into another 30 egg halves. Top these with slices of stuffed olive. Add the third mixture to the piping bag and fill the remaining egg halves. Top these with slices of black olive. Serve on a bed of finely shredded lettuce.

Note: This method ensures that there is no waste of the filling but you will find one or two egg halves may emerge parti-coloured where the fillings blend.

Mushroom and ham quiche: Line a 10 inch/25 cm flan ring with 12 oz/350 g shortcrust pastry. Chop 4 oz/100 g ham and place in the pastry case. Chop 8 oz/225 g mushrooms, sauté in 1 oz/25 g/2 tablespoons butter, then cool and sprinkle over the ham. Mix together $\frac{1}{2}$ pint/300 ml/1$\frac{1}{4}$ cups milk, 2 eggs and seasoning to taste and pour into the flan. Bake in a moderately hot oven (400°F, 200°C, Gas Mark 6) for 15 minutes, then reduce heat to moderate (350°F, 180°C, Gas Mark 4) for a further 25-30 minutes, until the filling is set. Cool, pack in foil or polythene bag, seal, label and freeze. To serve, defrost unwrapped. To serve hot, place still frozen but unwrapped on a baking sheet, defrost and reheat in a moderately hot oven (400°F, 200°C, Gas Mark 6) for 25-30 minutes.

New potato and green pea salad: Using 3 lb/1.5 kg frozen or cooked and peeled new potatoes, cut each potato into neat dice. Fold in 1 lb/450 g cooked frozen or fresh green peas and $\frac{3}{4}$ pint/400 ml/scant 2 cups mayonnaise. Serve garnished with green grapes and tomato wedges.

Rice and pepper salad: Using 1 lb/450 g long grain rice, cooked in chicken stock, fold in 12 oz/350 g blanched red and green pepper strips, 4 oz/100 g toasted flaked almonds and $\frac{1}{4}$ pint/150 ml/generous $\frac{1}{2}$ cup French dressing. Serve garnished with sprigs of watercress.

Chicken and pimiento aspic mould

INGREDIENTS	METRIC	IMP.	U.S.
Liquid aspic	600 ml	1 pint	2½ cups
Canned red pimiento	65 g	2½ oz	2½ oz
Cooked chicken, diced	450 g	1 lb	1 lb

Make up aspic according to directions with slightly less than 1 pint/generous ½ litre/2½ cups boiling water to ensure that the mould sets well. Cool. Drain the pimientoes and cut into diamond shapes. Pour about ½ inch/1 cm aspic into the bottom of a Tupperware Jel'N'Serve or 2 pint/generous 1 litre/5 cups mould. Arrange some pimiento shapes decoratively in this, and place in the refrigerator to set. Add about one third of the chicken (which should fill a 1 pint/generous ½ litre/2½ cups measuring jug, lightly packed). Cover with more aspic and allow to set. Arrange remaining pimiento shapes round sides, fill centre with chicken and pour over remaining aspic. The mould should be quite full. Turn out when set.

Creamy Dijon dip

INGREDIENTS	METRIC	IMP.	U.S.
Butter	25 g	1 oz	2 tbspn
3 tbspn flour			
1 chicken stock [bouillon] cube			
Boiling water	300 ml	½ pint	1¼ cups
1 tbspn vinegar			
3 tbspn Dijon mustard			
Cream cheese	75 g	3 oz	3 oz
2 tbspn cream			

Melt the butter in a small saucepan and stir in the flour. Cook for 2 minutes. Dissolve the stock cube in the boiling water, add to the roux and bring to the boil, stirring constantly until sauce is smooth and thick. Cook for 2 minutes. Cool. Mix together the vinegar and mustard and stir into the sauce. Beat the cream cheese and cream until smooth and gradually beat in the mustard mixture until well blended.
Serve with Chicken fingers in batter.

Spring fruit salad First make the liqueur syrup. Drain syrup from 2 large cans of fruit (peach slices, pineapple, etc.) and make up to 2 pints/generous 1 litre/5 cups with water. Dissolve 1½ lb/675 g sugar in the syrup and bring to the boil, stirring. Simmer for 2-3 minutes, add ¼ pint/150 ml/generous ½ cup fruit liqueur (Kirsch, Cointreau, Curaçao) and allow to cool. Chill before using. To make the fruit salad – peel and slice sufficient assorted fruits in season, such as apples, pears, bananas, strawberries, raspberries, peaches, apricots, cherries, plums, so that the proportion of fresh to canned fruit is four to one.

German wine cup Pour 300 ml/½ pint/1¼ cups fresh orange juice into a glass punch bowl. Add 6 tablespoons brandy, 2 bottles white Rhine wine and 1 litre/1¾ pints/4½ cups fizzy lemonade (soda). Float thin slices of orange, lemon and apple, and a few mint leaves on top.

Christmas catering for a family party
Serves 8–10

Christmas Eve
Gourmet's egg flip
Hors d'oeuvres speared on cocktail sticks
Spreads with savoury biscuits
Unusual hot hors d'oeuvres

Christmas dinner
Consommé starters
Roast turkey with
Original turkey stuffings
Cranberry orange sauce
Port wine jelly

Christmas Day supper
Cold roast turkey slices

Snow frosted ham
Celery sticks stuffed with cream cheese
Crispy rolls and butter

The sweets of Christmas
Light Christmas pudding
Marsala sauce
Hot rum sauce
Beat'n bake Christmas cake
Brandied mincemeat
Plum cake with rum syrup
Petits fours
Swiss roll with mincemeat cream
Glacé fruits

Every hostess cooks for compliments at Christmas, but not necessarily because hers are the best baked mince pies or the most evenly browned turkey. Once the festivities are over, most people have enjoyed their fill of traditional fare. Guests will welcome the originality of your catering if you offer a choice of these more unusual dishes and drinks.

Christmas Eve
When friends or relatives drop in on Christmas Eve, serve Gourmet's egg flip with an assortment of hot or cold hors d'oeuvres.

Gourmet's egg flip: For each serving beat one egg yolk with a tablespoon of sugar, 2 fl oz/50 ml double cream and 2 fl oz/50 ml rum, whisky or brandy. Fold in one stiffly beaten egg white and a few grains of salt. Sprinkle with cinnamon or nutmeg.

Hors d'oeuvres speared on cocktail sticks:
Avocado cubes dipped in lemon juice
Pineapple pieces and Camembert cheese cubes
Melon or cucumber fingers wrapped in paper-thin roast beef slices
Prawns dipped in curried mayonnaise
Apple wedges dipped in lemon juice with blue cheese cubes
Cheese cubes with pickled onions rolled in toasted breadcrumbs
Banana fingers dipped in lemon juice and rolled in chopped nuts
Small prunes stuffed with cream cheese (remove prune stones first)

Spreads for savoury biscuits:
Sardines mashed with lemon juice and sprinkled with paprika
Crumbled blue cheese on thin tomato slices spread with mayonnaise
Cream cheese sprinkled with chopped nuts
Chopped prawns and chicken livers garnished with capers
Camembert cheese and finely chopped dill pickle
Chopped prawns mixed with mayonnaise and topped with pineapple pieces
Tuna fish mashed with cream cheese and lemon juice
Minced ham and Dijon mustard

Unusual hot hors d'oeuvres:
Spread toast triangles with grated Cheddar cheese mixed with mayonnaise. Sprinkle with paprika pepper and grill until bubbly and brown
Heat contents of a small can of drained cocktail sausages in two tablespoons prepared mustard mixed with 4 tablespoons red currant jelly. Spear on cocktail sticks when hot
Spoon creamed chicken into small profiteroles and heat in a moderately hot oven (400°F, 200°C, Gas Mark 6) for 10 minutes
Add flaked crabmeat and sweet corn to cheese sauce and spoon into tiny vol-au-vent cases. Heat in a moderately hot oven (400°F, 200°C, Gas Mark 6) for 10 minutes or until heated through
Spread tuna fish mixed with mayonnaise and finely chopped celery on thinly sliced buttered bread. Roll up and slice into pinwheels. Chill, brush lightly with melted butter and grill until browned

Marinate chicken livers for one hour in soy sauce with a pinch of ginger and curry powder. Drain, wrap in bacon and thread on skewers. Grill until the bacon is cooked

Christmas dinner

For a light and refreshing start, serve consommé with a flair. Start with canned consommé, dilute with water if necessary and add one of the following:
A tablespoon of medium dry sherry or port
Crumbled cooked bacon and a pinch of curry powder
Chopped prawns and toasted almonds
Grated cucumber and a few drops of lime juice
Condensed tomato soup and a pinch of nutmeg
Garnish with slices of avocado

With the roast turkey: Serve Cranberry orange sauce or Port wine jelly.
Cranberry orange sauce: Cook 1 lb/450 g cranberries with 1 lb/450 g sugar and $\frac{1}{2}$ pint/300 ml/$1\frac{1}{4}$ cups orange juice until cranberry skins burst. Chill in refrigerator until firm.
Port wine jelly: Dissolve 1 lb/450 g sugar in $\frac{3}{4}$ pint/ 450 ml/2 cups port wine over gentle heat. Stir in 6 fl oz/ 200 ml/$\frac{3}{4}$ cup commercial pectin. Pour into a jelly

mould and chill until firm. Unmould on a glass dish.
Turkey stuffings: Try an original touch this year:
Substitute cooked long grain rice for the breadcrumbs in your usual stuffing recipe
Add dried apricots to bread or rice stuffing. (Soak the apricots in water, then chop finely)
Sauté sliced mushrooms in butter and add to bread stuffing
Add crumbled cooked bacon to bread stuffing
Add Madeira, sherry or apple brandy to chestnut stuffing

Christmas Day supper

For an easy and light Christmas Day supper: Serve cold sliced turkey, Snow frosted ham, which can be made the day before, celery sticks stuffed with cheese, and buttered rolls. Roll left-over turkey stuffing in foil, refrigerate, then slice and serve cold.

Snow frosted ham: Blend cream cheese with soured cream until spreading consistency. Beat in horse-radish, celery salt and black pepper to taste. Spread evenly over a cooked ham. Garnish with whole fresh cranberries and gherkin slices. Sprinkle with coarse salt. Refrigerate until required.

Light Christmas pudding

INGREDIENTS	METRIC	IMP.	U.S.
Soft [light] brown sugar	100 g	4 oz	½ cup
Plain [all-purpose] flour	200 g	7 oz	1¾ cups
1 tspn bicarbonate of soda [baking soda]			
½ tspn salt			
½ tspn ground cinnamon			
½ tspn grated nutmeg			
½ tspn ground mixed spices			
Seedless [dark seedless] raisins	100 g	4 oz	¾ cup
Currants	100 g	4 oz	⅔ cup
Sultanas [golden raisins]	100 g	4 oz	¾ cup
Chopped mixed peel	100 g	4 oz	1 cup +
Corn oil	65 ml	2½ fl oz	⅓ cup −
Milk	75 ml	3 fl oz	⅓ cup
4 tbspn brandy			
2 eggs			

Grease a 2 pint/1 litre/1 quart pudding basin and coat with brown sugar. Sieve the dry ingredients into a bowl and stir in the fruit. Whisk together the corn oil, milk, brandy and eggs and stir into the dry ingredients. Mix well. Turn into the prepared basin. Cover with greaseproof paper and foil and steam for 6 hours. Allow to cool. Remove the paper and recover with a clean dry cloth. When required steam for a further 1½ hours and serve with Marsala sauce, or Hot rum sauce.

Marsala sauce

INGREDIENTS	METRIC	IMP.	U.S.
Cornflour [cornstarch]	15 g	½ oz	1 tbspn
Milk	300 ml	½ pint	1¼ cups
2 tbspn sugar			
4 tbspn Marsala			
½ tspn almond essence [extract]			
Knob of butter			

Moisten the cornflour with 2 tablespoons of the milk. Heat the remaining milk gradually to boiling point with the sugar. Pour on to the blended cornflour, stir well and return to the pan. Bring to the boil again, stirring constantly. Add the Marsala and almond essence and simmer, stirring constantly, for a further 3 minutes. Beat in the butter and remove from the heat. Makes ½ pint/300 ml/1¼ cups sauce.

Hot rum sauce

INGREDIENTS	METRIC	IMP.	U.S.
Soft brown sugar	225 g	8 oz	1 cup
Honey	75 ml	3 fl oz	⅓ cup
Pinch salt			
Butter	100 g	4 oz	½ cup
Hot water	50 ml	2 fl oz	¼ cup
Rum	75 ml	3 fl oz	⅓ cup

In a small saucepan, heat the brown sugar, honey, salt, butter and water together until it begins to boil. Remove from the heat and stir in the rum. Makes ½ pint/300 ml/1¼ cups sauce.

Beat 'n bake Christmas cake

INGREDIENTS	METRIC	IMP.	U.S.
Mixed dried fruit	*450 g*	*1 lb*	*3 cups*
Chopped candied and glacé fruit	*125 g*	*4 oz*	*1 cup +*
Flour	*200 g*	*7 oz*	*1¾ cups*
1 tspn ground mixed spices (nutmeg, cinnamon, etc)			
Chopped almonds	*50 g*	*2 oz*	*½ cup*
Ground almonds	*50 g*	*2 oz*	*¼ cup +*
Soft margarine	*100 g*	*4 oz*	*½ cup*
Soft [light] brown sugar	*100 g*	*4 oz*	*½ cup*
2 tbspn treacle [molasses]			
3 large eggs			
1 miniature bottle Apricot brandy			

Quite simply, place all the ingredients together in a large mixing bowl and beat with a wooden spoon until too tired to continue (3 minutes is the minimum). Grease and line an 8 inch/20 cm cake tin and protect by wrapping a double layer of brown paper around the outside, to come 2 inches/5 cm above the top of the tin. Turn in the mixture, smooth the top and bake, standing on a pad of newspaper, in a cool oven (275°F, 150°C, Gas Mark 1), for about 3 hours, until no sound of humming is heard from the cake. Cool, and store in an airtight tin.

Note: A week before serving, cover the top of the cake with a layer of almond paste. A few days later, coat this with fondant icing (see page 29) and decorate as shown in the photograph opposite with chopped walnuts, maraschino cherries and holly leaves.

Brandied mincemeat

INGREDIENTS	METRIC	IMP.	U.S.
Cooking [baking] apples	*750 g*	*1½ lb*	*1½ lb*
Mixed candied peel	*225 g*	*8 oz*	*2 cups*
Blanched almonds	*100 g*	*4 oz*	*1 cup*
Glacé [candied] cherries	*225 g*	*8 oz*	*2 cups*
1 orange			
1 lemon			
Currants	*450 g*	*1 lb*	*2½ cups*
Seedless raisins	*450 g*	*1 lb*	*3 cups +*
Demerara [brown] sugar	*450 g*	*1 lb*	*2 cups*
Shredded [finely chopped] suet	*450 g*	*1 lb*	*2¾ cups*
½ tspn salt			
½ tspn mixed spice			
1 tspn grated nutmeg			
Brandy	*150 ml*	*¼ pint*	*½ cup*

Peel, core and chop apples. Finely chop the peel, almonds, and cherries. Grate the rind from the orange and lemon, and squeeze the juice. Stir all the ingredients together until well blended. Cover, and allow to stand for 2 days. Pack into clean jars and seal as for jam. Makes approximately 7 lb/3 kg.

Note: To make a finer mincemeat, put all the dried and candied fruit through the mincer. To make the flavour of your mincemeat even richer, small amounts of fruit liqueur and fortified wines can be used instead of part of the brandy, or the fruit juice. Add a little extra sugar when using mincemeat for cooking. Keeps well for one year, and requires at least 1 month to mature, otherwise a suety flavour may predominate.

Instead of icing your Christmas cake, glaze it immediately after baking with one of the following:
Golden syrup glaze – combine equal amounts of golden syrup and water. Simmer for a few minutes. Brush over the warm fruit cake. Decorate with candied fruit and nuts. Brush the glaze over the fruits. Return to the oven for 10 minutes.
Jelly glaze – brush warm fruit cake with melted redcurrant jelly or any other favourite jelly. Decorate with candied fruit and nuts. Return to the oven for 20 minutes.
Honey glaze – brush warm honey over the warm fruit cake. Decorate with candied fruits and nuts. Brush again with warm honey.

Plum cake with rum syrup

INGREDIENTS	METRIC	IMP.	U.S.
Plain [all-purpose] flour	100 g	4 oz	1 cup
½ tspn baking powder			
½ tspn salt			
Margarine	75 g	3 oz	6 tbspn
Castor [granulated] sugar	100 g	4 oz	½ cup
3 eggs			
½ tspn vanilla essence [extract]			
Chopped, stoned [pitted] prunes	75 g	3 oz	½ cup +
Chopped glacé [candied] cherries	75 g	3 oz	¾ cup
Chopped candied peel	75 g	3 oz	½ cup
Sultanas [golden raisins]	75 g	3 oz	½ cup +
Flaked [slivered] almonds	50 g	2 oz	¼ cup
SYRUP			
Granulated sugar	225 g	8 oz	1 cup
Water	300 ml	½ pint	1¼ cups
2 tbspn rum			
Glacé [candied] cherries and angelica to decorate			

Sieve the flour, baking powder and salt. Cream together the margarine and sugar until light and fluffy. Add one egg at a time, beating each in thoroughly. If mixture shows signs of curdling, beat in a little of the sieved flour. Beat in the vanilla essence. Fold in the flour, fruit and nuts. Turn the mixture into a well greased ring mould and bake in a cool oven (300°F, 150°C, Gas Mark 2) for 2½ hours. Remove from the oven and cool for 5 minutes before turning out. To make the syrup, dissolve the sugar in the water over gentle heat. Bring to the boil and continue boiling for 2 minutes. Remove from the heat and stir in the rum. Return the cake to the mould and prick the surface. Spoon over half the hot syrup and allow to stand for 30 minutes. Spoon more syrup over at intervals of one hour until it is all absorbed. Invert the cake on to a serving dish and decorate with cherries and angelica leaves.

Petits fours

INGREDIENTS	METRIC	IMP.	U.S.
Fresh or boxed whole dates	100 g	4 oz	1 cup
Marzipan [almond paste]	225 g	8 oz	$\frac{1}{2}$ lb
Red and green food colourings			
Plain [bitter] chocolate	100 g	4 oz	4 oz

Stone the dates. Keep aside two thirds of the marzipan and use the remaining third to roll into small shapes, the same size as the date stones and use to stuff the dates. Divide the remaining marzipan into three. Leave one third plain and colour the other two portions with red and green colouring respectively by patting out the marzipan, sprinkling with a few drops of the colouring and working this in by kneading it until paste is evenly coloured. Roll out all three pieces between your hands into ropes about 6 inches/15 cm long. Press two ropes close together on a board, and place the third rope between them on top. Make sure the different colours are firmly pressed together. Melt the chocolate in a basin over a pan of hot water. Pour over the marzipan roll, spread with a palette knife and allow to set. When quite dry, pass a palette knife under the roll to loosen it and cut into $\frac{1}{2}$ inch/1 cm slices diagonally with a sharp knife. Place the stuffed dates and marzipan slices in paper cases.

Swiss roll with mincemeat cream

INGREDIENTS	METRIC	IMP.	U.S.
3 large eggs			
Castor [granulated] sugar	100 g	4 oz	½ cup
Self-raising flour [all-purpose flour + 1 tspn baking powder]	75 g	3 oz	¾ cup
Melted butter	25 g	1 oz	2 tbspn
1 tbspn hot water			
FILLING			
Double [whipping] cream	300 ml	½ pint	1¼ cups
Mincemeat	225 g	8 oz	1 cup
Icing [confectioner's] sugar			

Line a swiss roll tin 9 inches/23 cm by 14 inches/35 cm with well greased greaseproof paper. Put the eggs and sugar into a basin and whisk hard until thick. Sieve the flour and fold in with a metal spoon, then fold in the butter and hot water. Pour mixture into the prepared tin and bake near the top of a hot oven (425°F, 220°C, Gas Mark 7) for 10 minutes. Sprinkle a sheet of greaseproof paper with icing sugar. When the roll is ready turn out onto the sugar and remove the paper. Put a clean sheet of greaseproof paper on top of the cake and roll up. Leave until cool. To make the filling whip the cream and mix gently with the mincemeat so the cream still holds its shape. Carefully unroll the cake and spread the filling over. Roll up and chill for 1 hour before serving. Dust with icing sugar.

Glacé fruits

INGREDIENTS	METRIC	IMP.	U.S.
1 seedless satsuma or clementine			
Sugar	75 g	3 oz	⅓ cup
3 tbspn water			
12 black [Tokay] grapes			

Peel the satsuma and divide into segments, removing as much white pith as possible. Place the sugar and water in a small saucepan and bring slowly to the boil making sure that the sugar dissolves before the mixture boils. Once sugar has dissolved do not stir. Boil until syrup just begins to turn pale straw colour. Immediately drop pieces of fruit one at a time into the syrup, removing with two skewers on to a board. Spoon any remaining syrup over the fruit before it sets. Place in paper sweet cases before completely cold and set to avoid them sticking to the board.

43

Family picnic party
Serves 8

Sausage and apple pielets
Filled celery sticks
Spiced chicken drumsticks

Fresh herb scones
Assorted cold meats
Frosty chocolate bananas

Sausage and apple pielets

INGREDIENTS	METRIC	IMP.	U.S.
Shortcrust pastry [basic pie dough]	450 g	1 lb	1 lb
1 medium cooking [baking] apple			
1 small onion			
Pork sausage meat [bulk pork sausage]	450 g	1 lb	1 lb
1 egg, beaten			

Roll out the pastry and use to line eight deep bun tins. Re-roll trimmings and cut out eight 3-inch/ 7.5 cm circles for lids. Grate the apple and onion and mix with the sausage meat. Divide the filling between the pastry cases, mounding it up well in the centres. Brush the edges of the pastry with a little beaten egg, place on the lids and crimp edges together with finger and thumb to seal. Add a little water to the remaining egg and brush over the tops of the pielets. Bake in a moderately hot oven (400°F, 200°C, Gas Mark 6) for 30 minutes, or until golden brown. Cool on a wire rack.

Filled celery sticks Remove all the outer sticks from a head of celery, wash and 'string' them to remove coarse outer fibres. Beat together 225 g/8 oz/½ lb curd cheese with 2 tablespoons chopped brown pickles and salt and pepper to taste. Press the mixture into the hollows of the sticks firmly and smooth the tops level. Cut into approximately 10 cm/4 inch lengths and pack in pairs with a divider between the filled surfaces.

Spiced chicken drumsticks Sprinkle 16 chicken drumsticks with a mixture of 2 tablespoons soy sauce, 1 tablespoon Worcestershire sauce and 1 teaspoon ground coriander. Cook under a hot grill, turning several times, and basting with the spicy mixture, for about 20 minutes, until cooked through. Cool and wrap in pairs in freezer film.

Frosty chocolate bananas

INGREDIENTS	METRIC	IMP.	U.S.
Plain [dark] chocolate	225 g	8 oz	½ lb
4 bananas			
Chopped peanuts	225 g	8 oz	1 cup

Melt the chocolate in a basin over a saucepan of hot water. Cut each banana in half crosswise and insert a wooden pick into the end of each banana half. Transfer the melted chocolate to a shallow dish. Roll the banana halves in the chocolate, and then in the chopped peanuts. Place on a tray lined with greaseproof paper and freeze until firm. Wrap individually in plastic cling wrap and return to the freezer. Makes 8.
Note: These will not melt for an hour at least if packed in an insulated bag.

Fresh herb scones

INGREDIENTS	METRIC	IMP.	U.S.
Wholemeal [wholewheat] flour	125 g	4 oz	1 cup
Plain [all-purpose] flour	125 g	4 oz	1 cup
½ tspn bicarbonate of soda [baking soda]			
1 tspn baking powder			
½ tspn salt			
Butter	50 g	2 oz	¼ cup
½ tspn dried mixed herbs			
2 tbspn chopped fresh herbs			
Natural [plain] yogurt	150 ml	¼ pint	½ cup +

Mix together the flours, bicarbonate of soda, baking powder and salt and rub in the butter. Stir in the remaining ingredients and knead to form a soft dough. Roll out lightly and cut into 2 inch/5 cm rounds. Place on greased baking trays and bake in a moderately hot oven (400°F, 200°C, Gas Mark 6) for 10-15 minutes, until golden brown. Serve split and buttered with slices of canned ox tongue, chopped ham and pork and party sausages.

Note: Don't forget to take the can opener and a suitable knife.

Elegant alfresco lunch Serves 8

Individual smoked salmon quiches
Avocado cream
Cervelat salad

Pippin salad
Smothered peaches

Individual smoked salmon quiches

INGREDIENTS	METRIC	IMP.	U.S.
Shortcrust pastry [basic pie dough]	450 g	1 lb	1 lb
Butter	25 g	1 oz	2 tbspn
2 medium onions, chopped			
Smoked salmon pieces	225 g	8 oz	$\frac{1}{2}$ lb
2 eggs			
Milk	300 ml	$\frac{1}{2}$ pint	$1\frac{1}{4}$ cups
Salt and pepper			

Roll out the pastry and use to line eight 4 inch/10 cm shaped foil flan cases. Chill. Melt the butter and use to fry the onion gently until soft. Chop the smoked salmon roughly, mix with the onion and divide between the pastry cases. Beat together the eggs and milk with seasoning to taste and pour over the filling. Bake in a moderately hot oven (400°F, 200°C, Gas Mark 6) for 25-30 minutes.

Avocado cream

INGREDIENTS	METRIC	IMP.	U.S.
2 large avocados			
French [Italian] dressing	6 tbspn	6 tbspn	7 tbspn
2 tbspn mayonnaise			
2 tbspn double [whipping] cream			
Juice of $\frac{1}{2}$ lemon			
Salt and pepper			

Peel the avocados, halve them, remove the stones and thinly slice the flesh. Place in a shallow dish with the dressing and allow to stand for 1 hour. Blend or mash until smooth and add the mayonnaise, lightly whipped cream and the lemon juice. Season to taste and beat well. Divide the mixture between 8 individual polythene containers, cover the surface with freezer film and seal them. Store in the refrigerator until ready to pack. Serve with Cervelat salad.

Smothered peaches

INGREDIENTS	METRIC	IMP.	U.S.
Sugar	350 g	12 oz	$1\frac{1}{2}$ cups
1 tspn almond essence [extract]			
8 large peaches			
Soured cream	300 ml	$\frac{1}{2}$ pint	$1\frac{1}{4}$ cups
Demerara [light brown] sugar	175 g	6 oz	$\frac{3}{4}$ cup
Toasted flaked [slivered] almonds	75 g	3 oz	1 cup

Dissolve the white sugar in $\frac{3}{4}$ pint/450 ml/2 cups water, add the almond essence and simmer for 5 minutes. Pour boiling water over the peaches to loosen the skins and remove them. Add the peaches to the syrup and poach for 7-8 minutes, according to the ripeness of the fruit. Remove from the heat and allow to cool. Take out the peaches, halve and remove the stones. Slice the peach halves and divide between 8 small polythene containers. Reduce the remaining syrup to $\frac{1}{4}$ pint/150 ml/generous $\frac{1}{2}$ cup and spoon over the fruit. Beat the soured cream until smooth and spread a layer over each dessert. Mix together the demerara sugar and toasted almonds and sprinkle thickly over the soured cream. Seal and chill until ready to pack.

Cervelat salad Chop 1 large mild onion very finely. Slice 3 long cervelat sausages or similar smoked sausages diagonally and put the slices in a shallow salad dish. Place 1 tablespoon wine vinegar, 2 tablespoons oil, a pinch of dry mustard, seasoning to taste and a crushed clove of garlic in a screw-topped jar and shake vigorously. Add the chopped onion and 1 tablespoon chopped parsley and pour over the sausage. Cover and chill for 1 hour before serving.

Pippin salad

INGREDIENTS	METRIC	IMP.	U.S.
3 eating apples			
1 celery heart			
1 small green pepper			
Few lettuce leaves			
Cream cheese	100 g	4 oz	½ cup
16 walnut halves			
Paprika pepper			
DRESSING			
Double [whipping] cream	150 ml	¼ pint	½ cup
1 tspn sugar			
½ tspn salt			
1 tbspn tarragon vinegar or lemon juice			
1 tspn French mustard			
Freshly ground black pepper			

First make the cream dressing. Mix together the cream, sugar and salt, then gradually add the vinegar or lemon juice, mustard and pepper to taste. Peel and core the apples and cut into small chunks. Chop the celery heart. Deseed and chop the pepper finely. Mix together the dressing, chopped apple, celery and pepper. Line a plastic bowl with lettuce leaves, and pile the apple mixture in the centre. Divide the cream cheese with a teaspoon into 8 small balls, press a walnut half into each side and use these to surround the salad. Sprinkle lightly with paprika pepper and cover.

Big barbecue party
Serves 12

Barbecue grilled sandwiches	Honeyed fruit kebabs
Jumbo beefburgers	Sweet afterthoughts:
Chilli barbecue sauce	Melba sauce
Cheesey frankfurters	Mocha sauce
Mexicali salad	Cart-wheel bananas
Liver sausage whip	Toasted coconut squares
Uncooked tomato chutney	

For entertaining without a fuss, plan a barbecue party . . . and be prepared for large appetites.

Light the fire at least 30 minutes before your guests arrive. To prepare the fire for a portable barbecue, line the base of the barbecue pan with foil and a layer of gravel. This makes cleaning up easier and provides ventilation for the fire. Pile the charcoal briquettes in the centre of the barbecue pan and set alight. Allow it to burn for 30 minutes or until the coals are covered with a grey ash. Arrange the coals over the base of the barbecue pan. Rub the grill rack with oil to prevent the food from sticking to it, and place it over the hot coals. Place the food on the grill so that pieces do not touch. Use long tongs to turn the food and keep a sprinkling can of water handy to douse flames from dripping fat. To keep the fire going, set extra charcoal briquettes around the edge of the barbecue pan to warm up before adding them to the fire. This will help to eliminate smoke from the fire.

Practically any of the meats you grill or fry in the kitchen can be cooked on the barbecue. Chops, steaks, sausages, frankfurters and beefburgers are favourites as they are quick-cooking and need little preparation.

Barbecue grilled sandwiches

INGREDIENTS	METRIC	IMP.	U.S.
Butter	100 g	4 oz	½ cup
Grated Cheddar cheese	175 g	6 oz	1½ cups
1 tspn hot mustard			
24 slices wholemeal bread			
12 slices cold boiled bacon			
Little oil			

Cream the butter and gradually mix in the cheese and mustard. Use this to spread one side of all the slices of bread. Top half the slices with boiled bacon, trimming it to fit neatly, then cover with the remaining slices of bread. Cut each sandwich in half diagonally and brush the outsides with oil. Barbecue the sandwiches until golden brown on both sides and the cheese filling is soft and melting.

Jumbo beefburgers

INGREDIENTS	METRIC	IMP.	U.S.
Minced [ground] beef	1 kg	2 lb	2 lb
1 large onion, finely chopped			
2 tspn salt			
¼ tspn pepper			
¼ tspn dry mustard			
3 tbspn ketchup [catsup]			
2 beaten eggs			

Mix the minced beef with the chopped onion, seasonings, ketchup and beaten eggs. Roll the mixture into 12 balls. Place the minced meat balls between squares of greaseproof paper and roll to ½ inch/1 cm thickness. Store in the refrigerator until required. Transport in insulated bag. To barbecue, place the beefburgers over hot coals and grill for 5 minutes on each side or until cooked through and nicely browned. Brush both sides of each beefburger frequently with Chilli sauce during cooking. Serve in buttered soft rolls.

48

Chilli barbecue sauce

INGREDIENTS	METRIC	IMP.	U.S.
1 large onion, finely chopped			
2 tbspn vinegar			
2 tbspn Worcestershire sauce			
1 tspn mild chilli powder			
Water	150 ml	$\frac{1}{4}$ pint	$\frac{2}{3}$ cup
Ketchup [catsup]	150 ml	$\frac{1}{4}$ pint	$\frac{2}{3}$ cup
3 tbspn cooking oil			

Place all the ingredients in a small saucepan. Cover and simmer for 15 minutes. Cool and store in a covered container in the refrigerator. Use as required. Makes $\frac{1}{2}$ pint/300 ml sauce.

Cheesey frankfurters

INGREDIENTS	METRIC	IMP.	U.S.
12 frankfurters			
Cheddar cheese	175 g	6 oz	6 oz
12 slices lean [back] bacon			
12 long rolls			
French mustard			

Cut a lengthwise slit down each frankfurter. Divide the cheese into 12 narrow pieces. Fill the slit in each frankfurter with a piece of cheese. Wrap the bacon securely around the frankfurters. Place over hot coals and grill until the bacon is crisp. Serve in rolls spread with mustard.

Mexicali salad

INGREDIENTS	METRIC	IMP.	U.S.
Carrots	450 g	1 lb	1 lb
White cabbage	450 g	1 lb	1 lb
1 green pepper, deseeded			
1 bunch spring onions [scallions]			
1 bunch radishes			
4 tomatoes			
French [Italian] dressing	300 ml	½ pint	1¼ cups

Shred the carrots and cabbage coarsely. Chop the green pepper and the onions. Slice the radishes and chop the tomatoes. Toss the prepared vegetables with the dressing. Refrigerate for 1 hour to blend the flavours.

Liver sausage whip

INGREDIENTS	METRIC	IMP.	U.S.
Liver sausage [liverwurst]	125 g	4 oz	¼ lb
Cream cheese	75 g	3 oz	3 oz
2 tbspn chopped parsley			
Double [whipping] cream	100 ml	4 fl oz	½ cup
Salt and pepper			

Mash the liver sausage until very smooth. Beat into the cream cheese. Stir in the chopped parsley. Whip the cream until thick and fold into the cheese mixture. Season to taste. Serve with potato crisps and small savoury biscuits.

Uncooked tomato chutney

INGREDIENTS	METRIC	IMP.	U.S.
Tomatoes	675 g	1½ lb	1½ lb
Peeled onions	450 g	1 lb	1 lb
Sultanas [golden raisins]	225 g	8 oz	1⅓ cups
Sugar	100 g	4 oz	½ cup
1 tbspn salt			
1 tbspn dry mustard			
¼ tspn ground ginger			
Vinegar			

Mince the tomatoes and onions and place in a bowl. Add the sultanas, sugar, salt, mustard and ginger and finally pour in vinegar to cover.

Out of the freezer the chutney will store for a limited period.

Honeyed fruit kebabs

INGREDIENTS	METRIC	IMP.	U.S.
Honey	250 ml	8 fl oz	1 cup
6 tbspn lemon juice			
Butter	100 g	4 oz	$\frac{1}{2}$ cup
4 eating apples, 4 pears, 2 small melons, 24 cherries			

First make the honey butter sauce. Combine the honey, lemon juice and butter in a saucepan and stir over heat until well blended. Dip wedges of unpeeled apples, fresh pears, melon cubes and cherries in the sauce. Thread alternately on long metal skewers and grill over a low fire until the fruit is glazed and heated through. Brush occasionally with the sauce and turn often to avoid scorching.

Sweet afterthoughts When the fire is getting low, serve barbecued desserts which require gentle heat, or set a pan on the grid to heat up a ready-made sauce to pour over ice cream or a cream layered cake.

Melba sauce This is a sauce which can be made with well sweetened raspberry purée. Heat 300 ml/$\frac{1}{2}$ pint/$1\frac{1}{4}$ cups raspberry purée (sieved if liked to remove the seeds) in a saucepan. Blend 1 tablespoon cornflour with 1 tablespoon water and stir into the purée. Cook over a low heat, stirring all the time, until the sauce thickens. Add 50 g/2 oz/$\frac{1}{4}$ cup castor sugar and the grated rind and juice of 1 lemon.

Mocha sauce Place 225 g/8 oz plain chocolate in the top of a double boiler, or a bowl placed over a pan of hot water, and heat until melted. Stir in 50 g/2 oz butter and 6 tablespoons strong black coffee. Mix together until the sauce is smooth and glossy.

Cart-wheel bananas Leave the peel on firm bananas. Cut in diagonal slices, about 1 inch/2.5 cm thick. Dip the cut ends in lemon juice, then coat with a mixture of brown sugar and cinnamon. Thread on long skewers, alternating with thick, unpeeled orange slices. Grill until the banana skin turns brown. Even the skins can be eaten.

Toasted coconut squares Dip 2 inch/5 cm squares of sponge cake into clear honey or sweetened condensed milk. Roll in desiccated coconut. Thread the cake pieces on long skewers and toast over the coals until the coconut turns golden.

Simple sausage barbecue party

Serves 12

Sweet and sour sausages
Caernarvon salad
Cheesey jacket potatoes

Sausages with barbecue sauce
Indian-style corn on the cob
Hot crusty rolls and butter

Cheesey jacket potatoes

INGREDIENTS	METRIC	IMP.	U.S.
12 even-sized potatoes			
Savoury white sauce	300 ml	½ pint	1¼ cups
Grated Cheddar cheese	175 g	6 oz	1½ cups
Salt and pepper			
4 tbspn chutney			

Wrap each potato separately in foil and bake in the coals of the barbecue until tender. Heat together the remaining ingredients in a pan and keep warm on the side of the barbecue. Split each cooked potato and pile with the cheese and chutney mixture. Serve piping hot.

Caernarvon salad

INGREDIENTS	METRIC	IMP.	U.S.
4 medium leeks			
1 lettuce			
6 medium tomatoes			
Small bunch radishes			
Double [whipping] cream	150 ml	¼ pint	⅔ cup
Mayonnaise	150 ml	¼ pint	⅔ cup
Salt and pepper			

Cut the leeks into 1 cm/½ inch slices, separate these into rings, place in a colander and wash well. Drain. Shred the lettuce, cut the tomatoes into wedges and trim and slice the radishes. Place all these together in a salad bowl. To make the dressing, whip the cream, combine with the mayonnaise until well blended and add seasoning to taste. Place in a bowl and serve separately with the salad.

Sweet and sour sausages

INGREDIENTS	METRIC	IMP.	U.S.
Sugar	175 g	6 oz	¾ cup
Vinegar	150 ml	¼ pint	⅔ cup
Water	75 ml	3 fl oz	⅓ cup
1 tbspn chopped green pepper			
1 tbspn chopped pimiento			
2 tspn cornflour [cornstarch]			
¼ tspn salt			
1 tspn paprika pepper			
12 beef or pork chipolatas [thin pork links]			

Combine the sugar, vinegar, water, chopped green pepper and pimiento in a small saucepan. Bring to the boil and simmer for 5 minutes. Moisten the cornflour and salt with a little cold water and slowly stir into the hot liquid. Cook, stirring constantly, until the sauce is thick. Cool, then add the paprika. Grill the sausages over hot coals, turning frequently and brushing with the sauce. Serve with toasted rolls and hand extra sauce separately.

Sausages with barbecue sauce

INGREDIENTS	METRIC	IMP.	U.S.
Sausages [pork links]	1.4 kg	2½ lb	2½ lb
6 mild onions			
BARBECUE SAUCE			
Ripe tomatoes	575 g	1¼ lb	1¼ lb
Cider or tarragon vinegar	120 ml	4 fl oz	½ cup
3 tbspn tomato ketchup [catsup]			
1 tbspn Worcestershire sauce			
3 bay leaves			
1-2 cloves garlic, chopped			
5 tbspn grated onion			
5 stalks celery, chopped			
1 medium lemon, sliced			
2 tbspn brown sugar			
Water	450 ml	¾ pint	2 cups
Salt and pepper			

First make the barbecue sauce. Peel the tomatoes and chop roughly. Place in a saucepan with all the other ingredients and bring to the boil. Cover and simmer gently for 30 minutes. Remove the bay leaves and lemon slices and adjust seasoning. Thread the sausages on long skewers with wedges of onion in between. Roast over a charcoal grill, turning frequently, until rich golden brown all over. Serve with hot crusty rolls, barbecue sauce and Indian style corn on the cob.

Indian-style corn on the cob

INGREDIENTS	METRIC	IMP.	U.S.
Allow 1 corn cob per person			
Butter per person	25 g	1 oz	2 tbspn
Salt and pepper			

Pull back the husks of each cob and remove the silky threads. Spread with softened butter, season with salt and pepper and re-fold husk leaves over cob. Thread each cob on a separate skewer and roast over charcoal, turning frequently. When the husks char, remove and cook the cobs until kernels are just golden. Serve on the skewers.

Summer buffet lunch Serves 8

Creamed prawn vol-au-vents
Poached salmon trout in aspic
Cucumber salad
Strawberry cream flans

Creamed prawn vol-au-vents

INGREDIENTS	METRIC	IMP.	U.S.
16 miniature vol-au-vent cases			
4 tbspn mayonnaise			
4 tbspn cool aspic jelly [½ tspn gelatin dissolved in 4 tbspn chicken broth]			
28 shelled prawns [large shrimp]			

Press down the centres of the vol-au-vent cases. Combine the mayonnaise and aspic jelly. Chop 12 of the shelled prawns and stir into the mayonnaise mixture. Use to fill the cases. Top each with a whole shelled prawn and a small sprig of parsley. Pile up on a serving dish and garnish with a few whole prawns in the shell.

Poached salmon trout in aspic

INGREDIENTS	METRIC	IMP.	U.S.
1 salmon trout			
Sprig of fennel			
Salt and pepper			
4 tbspn water			
Aspic jelly [gelatin dissolved in chicken broth]			

Gut the salmon trout leaving head and tail on. Place the sprig of fennel in the opening, season, enclose in foil. Place in a roasting tin containing the water. Cook in a moderate oven (350°F, 180°C, Gas Mark 4) for 45 minutes. Cool until warm, remove foil, place on serving dish, strip skin from uppermost side. Coat with cool aspic jelly. Decorate with sliced radishes, olives and cucumber, then coat again with jelly.

Strawberry cream flans

INGREDIENTS	METRIC	IMP.	U.S.
2 eggs, separated + 2 egg yolks			
Icing sugar, sifted	100 g	4 oz	1 cup
Self-raising flour [all-purpose flour + 2½ tspn baking powder]	250 g	9 oz	2¼ cups
Melted butter	125 g	4 oz	½ cup
Halved strawberries	450 g	1 lb	1 lb
PASTRY CREAM			
4 egg yolks			
Flour	50 g	2 oz	½ cup
Castor [granulated] sugar	125 g	4 oz	½ cup
Milk	600 ml	1 pint	2½ cups
Butter	50 g	2 oz	¼ cup
½ tspn vanilla essence [extract]			

Beat the 4 egg yolks with the sugar until pale and thick. Fold in the flour and the melted butter. Beat the egg whites stiffly and fold into the mixture. Pour into a greased 10 inch/25 cm fluted flan tin and bake in a moderate oven (350°F, 180°C, Gas Mark 4) for 35-45 minutes. Turn out on a wire rack to cool. To make the pastry cream, beat together the egg yolks, flour and sugar. Heat the milk to boiling boint, pour over the mixture and beat well. Return to the saucepan and bring to the boil, stirring constantly, until the mixture is smooth and thickened. Remove from the heat and beat in the butter and vanilla essence. Cool. Split the cake in half and place each half on a serving plate. Press down the soft inside with a metal spoon, fill each half with cream and top with the halved strawberries. Makes 2 flans.

Candlelight buffet supper Serves 8

Cheddar mushroom caps
Scalloped eggs
Peanut dip with crackers, celery and carrot sticks
Hawaiian pork cubes

Oven-baked rice
Quick tuna curry
Chocolate Viennese torte
Hazelnut cream gâteau
Cardamom coffee

This kind of informal gathering is so much more enjoyable than the unimaginative cocktail party, it is well worth the trouble of providing at least one hot dish for your guests.

Place the Peanut dip in the centre of a large round tray and surround with cold finger hors d'oeuvre – olives, gherkins, pickled onions, carrot and celery sticks, Cheddar mushroom caps, Scalloped eggs, and potato crisps. Keep the Quick tuna curry, Hawaiian pork cubes and Oven-baked rice hot on a warming tray or over candle warmers. If desired, serve hot garlic bread with the main course.

Cheddar mushroom caps

INGREDIENTS	METRIC	IMP.	U.S.
Button mushrooms	450 g	1 lb	1 lb
Chicken stock [broth]	300 ml	½ pint	1¼ cups
Butter	50 g	2 oz	¼ cup
Grated Cheddar cheese	75 g	3 oz	¾ cup
½ tspn Worcestershire sauce			
Pinch pepper			
2 tbspn chopped walnuts			

Toss the mushrooms lightly in simmering stock for 3 minutes. Drain, and remove the stems. Beat together the butter, cheese, Worcestershire sauce and pepper. Pipe the cheese mixture into the mushroom cavities and sprinkle with chopped walnuts. Chill. To serve, spear on cocktail sticks.

Scalloped eggs

INGREDIENTS	METRIC	IMP.	U.S.
8 hard-boiled eggs			
2 tbspn soured cream			
1 tspn prepared mustard			
Salt and pepper			
·16 ham cubes, each	1 cm	½ inch	½ inch

Cut the eggs in half crosswise and cut a thin slice off the base of each egg white half so they stand upright. Scoop out the yolk and mash with the soured cream and mustard. Season to taste with salt and pepper. Serrate the edges of the egg white halves and spoon the egg yolk filling into each half. Spear the ham cubes on cocktail sticks and spear through each filled egg half.

Peanut dip

INGREDIENTS	METRIC	IMP.	U.S.
Natural [plain] yogurt	150 ml	¼ pint	½ cup
Cottage [creamed cottage] cheese	100 g	4 oz	½ cup
Few drops Worcestershire sauce			
Pinch pepper			
Peanuts	100 g	4 oz	1 cup

Blend the yogurt, cottage cheese, Worcestershire sauce and pepper until smooth. Coarsely chop the peanuts and stir into the yogurt mixture. Chill well before serving. Serve with potato crisps, savoury biscuits, celery and carrot sticks.

Hawaiian pork cubes

INGREDIENTS	METRIC	IMP.	U.S.
Cooked lean pork	450 g	1 lb	1 lb
2 eggs			
Flour	25 g	1 oz	$\frac{1}{4}$ cup
1 tspn salt			
$\frac{1}{4}$ tspn pepper			
Fat for frying			
4 stalks celery			
2 tbspn cooking oil			
3 tbspn cornflour [cornstarch]			
White sugar	125 g	4 oz	$\frac{1}{2}$ cup
3 tbspn soy sauce			
White vinegar	150 ml	$\frac{1}{4}$ pint	$\frac{1}{2}$ cup
2 chicken stock [bouillon] cubes			
Hot water	300 ml	$\frac{1}{2}$ pint	$1\frac{1}{4}$ cups
Canned pineapple pieces	225 g	8 oz	8 oz
Parsley sprigs			
Freshly grated coconut			

Cut the cooked pork into 1 inch/2.5 cm cubes. In a large bowl, beat together the eggs, flour, salt and pepper. Toss the pork cubes in the batter until coated. Fry the pork cubes in hot deep fat until crisp and brown. Drain well and keep warm. Slice the celery diagonally and sauté in the oil until just tender, about 10 minutes. Mix the cornflour with the sugar, soy sauce and vinegar. Dissolve the chicken stock cubes in the hot water and stir into the cornflour mixture. Pour the sauce over the celery and cook until thick, stirring constantly. Stir in the drained pineapple pieces and pork cubes. Heat through, stirring gently. Garnish with parsley sprigs. Hand freshly grated coconut separately.

Oven-baked rice

INGREDIENTS	METRIC	IMP.	U.S.
Long grain rice	450 g	1 lb	$2\frac{2}{3}$ cups
2 tspn salt			
$\frac{1}{4}$ tspn white pepper			
Boiling water	1.15 litres	2 pints	5 cups
8 lemon wedges			
Paprika pepper			

Put the rice, salt and pepper into a lightly buttered ovenproof casserole. Pour the boiling water over the rice. Cover tightly and bake in a moderate oven (350°F, 180°C, Gas Mark 4) for 40-50 minutes. Dip the edge of each lemon wedge in paprika. Arrange the lemon wedges on the baked rice.

Candlelight buffet

Quick tuna curry

INGREDIENTS	METRIC	IMP.	U.S.
2 eating apples			
1 large onion			
Butter	50 g	2 oz	$\frac{1}{4}$ cup
Plain flour	25 g	1 oz	$\frac{1}{4}$ cup
2-3 tspn curry powder			
1 tspn salt			
Milk	900 ml	$1\frac{1}{2}$ pints	$3\frac{3}{4}$ cups
2 cans tuna fish, each	184 g	$6\frac{1}{2}$ oz	$6\frac{1}{2}$ oz
Toasted flaked [slivered] almonds	25 g	1 oz	$\frac{1}{4}$ cup

Peel and finely chop the apples and onion. Sauté in the butter until soft. Stir in the flour, curry powder and salt and cook for 2-3 minutes. Gradually add the milk and cook until thickened, stirring constantly. Drain the tuna fish well and break into chunks. Add the tuna to the sauce and heat through. Toast the almonds in a moderate oven (350°F, 180°C, Gas Mark 4) until lightly browned. Sprinkle the toasted almonds over the tuna curry just before serving.

Chocolate Viennese torte

INGREDIENTS	METRIC	IMP.	U.S.
Butter	225 g	8 oz	1 cup
Castor [granulated] sugar	225 g	8 oz	1 cup
5 eggs, beaten			
Plain [cake] flour	225 g	8 oz	2 cups
$\frac{1}{4}$ tspn ground nutmeg			
1 tspn vanilla essence [extract]			
FILLING			
Chocolate chips	175 g	6 oz	1 cup
Butter	125 g	4 oz	$\frac{1}{2}$ cup
2 tbspn water			
2 tbspn Crème de Caçao			
4 egg yolks			
2 tbspn icing [confectioner's] sugar			
Chopped nuts	50 g	2 oz	$\frac{1}{2}$ cup

First make the cake. Cream the butter and sugar together until light and fluffy. Gradually add the eggs and beat with an electric mixer for about 10 minutes. Fold in the flour, spice and vanilla essence. Pour into a greased 2 lb/1 kg loaf tin and bake in a moderate oven (325°F, 170°C, Gas Mark 3) for $1\frac{1}{4}$ hours. Turn out and cool on a wire rack. Meanwhile, combine the chocolate chips, butter, water and Crème de Caçao in a heavy saucepan and heat until blended. Cool to lukewarm. Lightly beat the egg yolks with the sugar and stir into the chocolate mixture. Chill for 1 hour, then beat until spreading consistency. Slice the cake horizontally into 6 layers. Spread the chocolate icing between each layer and on the top and sides of the cake. Sprinkle the chopped nuts on the top of the cake. Chill several hours before serving.

Hazelnut cream gâteau

INGREDIENTS	METRIC	IMP.	U.S.
Butter	100 g	4 oz	$\frac{1}{2}$ cup
Castor [granulated] sugar	100 g	4 oz	$\frac{1}{2}$ cup
2 eggs, beaten			
Self-raising flour [all-purpose flour + 1 tspn baking powder]	100 g	4 oz	1 cup
Pinch salt			
Chopped hazelnuts	50 g	2 oz	$\frac{1}{2}$ cup
Few hazelnut kernels			
Double [whipping] cream	300 ml	$\frac{1}{2}$ pint	$1\frac{1}{4}$ cups
Greengage jam	225 g	8 oz	1 cup

Cream the butter and sugar until light and fluffy. Gradually beat in the eggs, adding a teaspoon of flour with the last addition. Sieve the flour and salt and fold into the creamed mixture. Divide between two greased 7 inch/18 cm sandwich tins and bake in a moderate oven (350°F, 180°C, Gas Mark 4) for 25-30 minutes. Cool on a wire rack. Place the chopped and whole hazelnuts on a sheet of foil and toast under a hot grill until brown. Whip the cream until thick. Spread jam on one sponge layer and cover with a little of the cream. Place the other sponge layer on top and carefully spread a thin layer of cream over the sides of the cake. Press chopped hazelnuts against the sides to coat. Cover the top of the cake with greengage jam. Place remaining cream in a piping bag fitted with a star nozzle and pipe lines of cream evenly across the cake. Pipe rosettes around the edge of the cake and top each rosette with a whole hazelnut.

Note: The recipe can be varied by using other kinds of jam such as seedless raspberry.

Cardamom coffee

INGREDIENTS	METRIC	IMP.	U.S.
Boiling water	1.5 litres	$2\frac{1}{2}$ pints	6 cups
4 tbspn instant coffee granules			
1 tspn ground cardamom			
Double [whipping] cream	150 ml	$\frac{1}{4}$ pint	$\frac{1}{2}$ cup

Pour the boiling water over the instant coffee and cardamom. Pour into coffee cups and spoon lightly whipped double cream on top.

Party drinks for children

Florida flip
Grapefruit soda pop
Family fruit cup
Devon cup
Cola fancy
Chocolate challenger

Grapefruit glory
Peppermint twist
Iced coffee
Chocolate slim shake
Orange marvel

Hot summer days definitely call for cold drinks. Sometimes children demand so many fizzy drinks you feel they might burst or float away! These drinks are filling in a tummy-distending sense, but have nothing important to offer in the form of nutrition. How about giving the younger members of the family and their friends a choice of these thirst-quenchers, all high in excellent nutritive value? Frozen fruit juice concentrates take little space to store in the fridge or freezer and when made up one is pleasantly surprised by the quantity these convenient cans produce.

Good for all the family

Florida flip: Make up 1 can frozen Florida orange juice as directed on the can. Place in a bowl and whisk in 1 egg and 1 rounded tablespoon clear honey. Serves 6.

Grapefruit soda pop: Place a small cube of ice cream in the base of each of 8 tall glasses. Make up 1 can frozen Florida grapefruit juice as directed on the can and use to half-fill the tumblers. Top up with a whoosh of soda water (club soda) and drop a pineapple cube into each glass. Long-handled spoons are useful for reaching the goodies in the glasses! Serves 8.

Family fruit cup: Make up 1 can frozen Florida orange juice as directed on the can. Mix with 600 ml/1 pint/ 2½ cups cold weak tea and 600 ml/1 pint/2½ cups ginger ale. Chill well and serve in a bowl with slices of strawberry, orange and cucumber, and sprigs of mint floating on the top. Serves about 10.

Devon cup: Mix together 150 ml/¼ pint/½ cup orange juice and 600 ml/1 pint/2½ cups apple juice. Chill well then add 600 ml/1 pint/2½ cups fizzy lemonade (7 up) just before serving. Serves 6.

Super singles

Cola fancy: Place ice cubes in a glass and pour over 125 ml/4 fl oz/½ cup orange juice and 50 ml/2 fl oz/ ¼ cup cola. Serve with a slice of orange over the side of the glass.

Chocolate challenger: Drop a few cubes of ice and 6 little chunks of chocolate ice cream into a glass containing 125 ml/4 fl oz/½ cup orange juice. Sprinkle with drinking chocolate powder.

Grapefruit glory: Place half a ripe banana and 125 ml/ 4 fl oz/½ cup grapefruit juice in a blender and liquidize until smooth. Pour into a glass and top up with fizzy lemonade (7 up).

Peppermint twist: Place 4 teaspoons drinking chocolate powder in a mug and add just sufficient boiling water to dissolve. Cool and fill the mug with cold milk. Stir well and add a drop or two of peppermint essence to taste. For a festive occasion, decorate the top with a swirl of cream and 2 chocolate drops.

Slimmer's delight

Even tubby toddlers yearn for long drinks which are more exciting than a plain glass of fruit juice or cordial. By using low calorie ingredients, you can make up some exotic alternatives for occasional use very simply. Try one of these.

Iced coffee: Measure 1 teaspoon instant coffee into a jug and add a small teaspoon of honey. Stir in just sufficient boiling water to dissolve the ingredients. Add 300 ml/½ pint/1¼ cups liquid skimmed milk and chill well. Serve over ice cubes in a tall glass.

Chocolate slim shake: Dissolve 1 tablespoon drinking chocolate powder in a very little boiling water, then cool. Spoon 2 tablespoons dry skimmed milk powder into a glass, add the dissolved drinking chocolate and gradually stir in low calorie fizzy lemonade (7 up) to fill the glass.

Orange marvel: Whisk 2 tablespoons undiluted low calorie orange squash (concentrate) into 150 ml/ ¼ pint/½ cup liquid skimmed milk. Add about 25 g/ 1 oz/2 tablespoons vanilla ice cream, cut up into chunks. Stir well and pour into a long glass. Decorate with a slice of orange.

Children's tea party

Serves 8

Bow ties
Rolled pineapple sandwiches
Fruity orange baskets
Mandarin wedges
Banana candles

Bow ties

INGREDIENTS	METRIC	IMP.	U.S.
Puff pastry [paste]	350 g	12 oz	¾ lb
2 Cubes from Bovril or beef stock [bouillon] cubes			
Grated Cheddar cheese	100 g	4 oz	1 cup
Beaten egg			

Roll out the pastry thinly to a rectangle measuring 25 cm/10 inches by 20 cm/8 inches. Divide in half down the longer length. Crumble the stock cubes and mix with the cheese. Sprinkle over one piece of pastry and top with the other piece. Press lightly and cut into 16 strips measuring 2.5 cm/1 inch by 6.5 cm/2½ inches. Twist each strip once in the centre to make a 'bow tie' and place them well apart on a greased baking sheet. Brush with the egg and bake in a hot oven (425°F, 220°C, Gas Mark 7) for about 12 minutes, until well puffed up and golden brown. Serve warm. Makes 16.

Rolled pineapple sandwiches

INGREDIENTS	METRIC	IMP.	I.S.
Butter	50 g	2 oz	¼ cup
½ Cube from Bovril or beef stock [bouillon] cube			
8 slices fresh brown bread			
Cream cheese	75 g	3 oz	3 oz
8 drained fingers canned pineapple			

Cream the butter with the crumbled stock cube. Remove the crusts from the bread. Spread the slices first with savoury butter then with the cream cheese. Place a finger of pineapple on the edge of each slice and roll up like a Swiss roll (jelly roll). Secure each with a wooden cocktail stick (toothpick) and chill well. Remove sticks before serving. Makes 8.

Fruity orange baskets

INGREDIENTS	METRIC	IMP.	U.S.
4 large oranges			
Drained canned fruit cocktail	450 g	1 lb	2 cups
8 25 cm/10 inch lengths narrow red ribbon			

Cut the oranges in half and trim a tiny piece off the rind if necessary, so that all eight halves will sit firmly on a plate. To make the baskets, slice almost halfway through across the cut side of each orange half, about 1 cm/¼ inch down on both sides, leaving only a small portion of the skin uncut. Scoop out most of the orange flesh, chop and mix with the fruit cocktail. Bring up the two loops of orange skin and fix together firmly in the centre with a piece of clear adhesive tape. Cover the join with a ribbon bow. Carefully fill the baskets with the fruit cocktail mixture. (You will find it easier to do this after tying the bows.)

Mandarin wedges Drain the syrup from a 202 g/
7½ oz can mandarin oranges. Make up to 150 ml/
¼ pint/⅔ cup with water. Use to dissolve an orange
jelly (3½ oz package orange gelatin). When setting,
whisk in 4 tablespoons evaporated milk. Fold in
mandarins. Set in a rinsed shallow cake tin. Turn out
and serve in wedges. Decorate as liked.

Banana candles

INGREDIENTS	METRIC	IMP.	U.S.
4 straight bananas			
Canned mandarin oranges	325 g	11 oz	11 oz
8 drained canned pineapple rings			
8 tbspn double [whipping] cream			
8 narrow 10 cm/4 inch strips angelica			
1 small piece red-skinned apple			

Halve the bananas and drain the mandarins.
Place each pineapple ring on a small serving
plate. Whip the cream and pipe a little into the
hole in the centre of each and insert half a
banana, cut side down, so that it stands up
straight to form the candle. Arrange mandarin
segments round the outer edge of the pineapple
slice to finish off the candlestick base. Rinse
each angelica strip in warm water to make it
pliable and insert one end down the side of a
candle and tuck the other under the edge of the
candlestick base, to form the handle. Place a
blob of cream on top of each candle and press in
a tiny piece of cut apple (or a cherry from canned
fruit cocktail) to make the flame.

Pancake party Serves 8

Crab and sweetcorn pancakes
Sausage and cheese pancakes
Cottage cheese pancakes

Basic pancakes

INGREDIENTS	METRIC	IMP.	U.S.
Plain [all purpose] flour	100 g	4 oz	1 cup
Pinch salt			
1 egg			
Milk or	300 ml	½ pint	1¼ cups
Milk and	175 ml	6 fl oz	¾ cup
Water	125 ml	4 fl oz	½ cup
Oil and butter for frying			

Sieve the flour and salt into a bowl. Make a well in the centre and add the egg. Beat well. Combine the milk and water. Add half of the liquid and beat for 2 minutes. Beat in the remaining liquid. Mix a little softened butter and oil together in equal proportions. Lightly grease a small omelette or frying pan. Heat until a drop of water 'sizzles' on the surface. Pour sufficient batter into the pan to cover the base thinly. Allow the pancake to brown on one side, turn over and brown the other side. Transfer the cooked pancake to a warm plate. Continue to prepare the pancakes, re-greasing the pan when necessary, until all the batter is used. Makes 8-10 pancakes.

To keep the pancakes hot, place in an uncovered dish in a warm oven or over a pan of boiling water. If the pancakes are to be used later in the day, separate each with a layer of greaseproof paper and place in the refrigerator until required.

For a richer pancake: Use 2 eggs and all milk. Add 1 tablespoon oil or melted butter to the batter before cooking for a crisper pancake.

Crab and sweetcorn pancakes

INGREDIENTS	METRIC	IMP.	U.S.
Canned sweetcorn kernels	200 g	7 oz	1 cup
Fresh or frozen crab meat	225 g	8 oz	½ lb
Béchamel [savory white] sauce	250 ml	8 fl oz	1 cup
Salt and pepper			
8 pancakes			
Grated Gruyère [Swiss] cheese	25 g	1 oz	¼ cup
Parsley sprigs			

Drain the sweetcorn and flake the crab meat. Fold these into the béchamel sauce and season to taste with salt and pepper. Divide the filling between 8 pancakes. Fold in half twice to make triangles and place in a shallow baking dish. Sprinkle the grated cheese over the filled pancakes. Bake in a moderately hot oven (400°F, 200°C, Gas Mark 6) for 20 minutes. Garnish with the parsley sprigs.

Sausage and cheese pancakes

INGREDIENTS	METRIC	IMP.	U.S.
Pork sausage meat [bulk pork sausage]	225 g	8 oz	½ lb
1 small onion			
Grated Cheese	50 g	2 oz	¼ cup
Cream cheese	75 g	3 oz	3 oz
¼ tspn dried marjoram			

Brown the sausage meat and drain some of the fat. Chop the onion finely and fry with the sausage meat until limp, but not brown. Drain off excess fat. Remove from the heat and stir in the grated cheese, cream cheese and dried marjoram. Chill the filling in the refrigerator until required. Divide the sausage filling among 8 pancakes. Roll up and place the filled pancakes in a shallow baking dish. Cover and bake in a moderately hot oven (375°F, 190°C, Gas Mark 5) for 30 minutes. Remove the cover and bake for a further 5 minutes.

Cottage cheese pancakes

INGREDIENTS	METRIC	IMP.	U.S.
Cottage cheese	450 g	1 lb	2 cups
1 egg			
Pinch salt			
2 tbspn castor [granulated] sugar			
8 pancakes			

Mix all the filling ingredients until well blended Store in the refrigerator until required. Divide the filling among 8 pancakes, roll up and place the filled pancakes in a shallow ovenproof dish. Cover lightly with foil and bake in a moderately hot oven (375°F, 190°C, Gas Mark 5) for 20 minutes.

More about pancakes

Baked layered pancakes: Alternatively, the same fillings can be used in a layered pancake casserole. Lightly grease an ovenproof casserole the diameter of the cooked pancakes. Place a pancake in the base of the dish, spoon some filling over, then place another pancake on top. Continue to alternate pancakes and filling to within 1 inch/2.5 cm of the top of the dish. Cover with a complementary sauce – tomato sauce over the sausage and cheese filling, béchamel sauce over the crab and sweetcorn filling, or coffee sauce over the cottage cheese filling. Cover and bake in a moderately hot oven (400°F, 200°C, Gas Mark 6) for 30 minutes. Remove the cover and bake 5 minutes longer. Serve cut into wedges.

Savoury pancakes: For variety, especially at breakfast or lunchtime, add one of the following to the basic pancake batter and cook as directed.
4 oz/100 g/¾ cup diced cooked ham. Serve the ham pancakes with grilled pineapple slices.
2 oz/50 g/½ cup crumbled cooked bacon. Serve bacon pancakes with scrambled eggs for breakfast
2 oz/50 g grated cheese. Roll the cheese pancakes around grilled frankfurters. Sprinkle with some more grated cheese and brown under the grill
Substitute wholemeal flour for the plain flour. Serve with butter and blue cheese

Decrease the flour to 2 oz/50 g/½ cup and the milk to 8 fl oz/225 ml/1 cup. Add 4 oz/100 g/1 cup cooked long grain rice to the batter

Sweet pancakes: Follow the basic recipe or use the richer variation, and add 2 tablespoons sugar to the flour. The simplest way of serving sweet pancakes is to dust liberally with extra sugar and sprinkle with lemon juice. Try adding one of the following to the batter for a pleasant change:
4 oz/100 g/1 cup grated raw apple, pinch of cinnamon and nutmeg. Serve with maple syrup
Drained, chopped, canned fruit such as peaches, pears, apricots or pineapple pieces
Fresh blueberries, sliced strawberries or sliced bananas. Serve with whipped sweetened cream

½ teaspoon grated orange rind. Substitute 4 fl oz/125 ml/½ cup of the liquid with 4 fl oz/125 ml/½ cup sweetened orange juice. Serve with canned mandarin orange segments and orange flavoured yogurt
2 oz/50 g melted plain chocolate (decrease liquid by 2 fl oz/50 ml/¼ cup). Serve with ice cream
2 oz/50 g/⅓ cup desiccated coconut. Serve with pineapple pieces and rum butter
1 oz/25 g/¼ cup chopped candied ginger. Serve with soured cream and brown sugar.
Or roll the sweet pancakes around any of these fillings:
Apple purée spiced with cinnamon
Banana halves; dust the rolled pancakes with demerara sugar and place under the grill for a few minutes to glaze.
Strawberry or raspberry purée blended into whipped double cream.
Sliced peaches; serve with hot strawberry jam sauce
Mincemeat; serve with brandy or rum butter.

Freezing pancakes ahead of time: This is an excellent idea to ensure a good supply for quickly-made sweet and savoury dishes. Cook them in the usual way and stack up with dividers of foil or greaseproof paper to prevent them from sticking together. Wrap in a foil parcel and freeze. When required, unwrap, defrost and separate. This will take about 1 hour. Spread with a tasty mixture such as crab paste mixed with chopped prawns. Lightly fold the pancakes in four or roll them. Arrange in a shallow baking dish and sprinkle with grated cheese. Bake in a moderately hot oven (375°F, 190°C, Gas Mark 5) until heated through and the cheese begins to melt. Sweet fillings are just as successful. Canned cherry or apricot pie fillings are particularly good and the pancakes can be sprinkled with chopped almonds before baking. Sift icing (confectioner's) sugar over them at serving time. If you enjoy Crêpes Suzette, a quick version can be made by spreading the pancakes with marmalade and reheating in a shallow pan, folded in four, in a rich sauce made with orange juice and a spoonful or two of orange-flavoured liqueur, such as Curaçao.

Cinnamon honey butter

INGREDIENTS	METRIC	IMP.	U.S.
Softened butter	*100 g*	*4 oz*	*½ cup*
4 tbspn clear honey			
1 tspn ground cinnamon			

Mix all the ingredients until well blended. Serve with hot griddlecakes.

American griddlecakes

INGREDIENTS	METRIC	IMP.	U.S.
Plain [all-purpose] flour	175 g	6 oz	1½ cups
1 tspn salt			
1½ tspn baking powder			
2 eggs			
Milk	300 ml	½ pint	1¼ cups
2 tbspn oil			

Sieve the flour, salt and baking powder into a bowl. Beat the eggs until light. Make a well in the centre of the flour mixture and add the beaten eggs, milk and oil. Stir lightly. The batter will seem lumpy, but the lumps will disappear during cooking. Pour a little batter on to a greased hot griddle or frying pan. Allow to brown on one side. Turn over when bubbles form on the un-baked surface. Brown on the other side. Makes 12 medium-sized griddlecakes. Serve with maple syrup and peanuts, golden syrup or cinnamon honey butter.

French flan party

Serves 8

French onion and leek flan
Prawn and bacon flans
Mocha meringue flans
Orange gingerbread fingers
Café Napoléon

French onion and leek flan

INGREDIENTS	METRIC	IMP.	U.S.
4 small leeks			
2 large onions			
1 clove garlic			
Butter	*75 g*	*3 oz*	*⅓ cup*
Salt and pepper			
½ tspn dried marjoram			
Pale ale [light beer]	*450 ml*	*¾ pint*	*2 cups*
Grated Gruyère cheese	*75 g*	*3 oz*	*¾ cup*
PÂTE BRISÉE			
Plain [all purpose] flour	*225 g*	*8 oz*	*2 cups*
Pinch salt			
Butter	*100 g*	*4 oz*	*½ cup*
1 egg			
3 tbspn water			

To make the pâte brisée, sieve the flour and salt into a bowl, make a well in the centre, add the butter, egg and water and work into a paste, gradually drawing in all the flour. Knead well until smooth and silky. Wrap in foil and chill for 30 minutes. Roll out and use to line a large flan tin. Cut the leeks into 2 inch/5 cm lengths, halve and wash thoroughly. Cut the onions in thin slices and crush the garlic. Cook all together gently in the butter, stirring constantly over low heat for 5 minutes, until limp. Season with salt, pepper, marjoram and pour in the ale. Cover and cook gently until the liquid is well reduced and the vegetables cooked. Stir in the grated cheese and remove from the heat. Spread mixture in the prepared pastry case and bake in a moderate oven (350°F, 180°C, Gas Mark 4) for 25-30 minutes.

Prawn and bacon flans

INGREDIENTS	METRIC	IMP.	U.S.
Double quantity pâte brisée [see recipe opposite]			
Lean bacon	225 g	8 oz	$\frac{1}{2}$ lb
Peeled prawns [large shrimp]	350 g	12 oz	2 cups
4 eggs			
Milk	600 ml	1 pint	$2\frac{1}{2}$ cups
Salt and pepper			
Pinch ground nutmeg			
Sprigs of parsley			

Roll out the pastry and use to line two large flan tins. Derind the bacon and cut into strips. Grill until crisp. Arrange the bacon and shellfish evenly in the pastry cases. Beat together the eggs and milk and season with the salt, pepper and nutmeg. Pour carefully into the pastry cases and bake in a moderately hot oven (400°F, 200°C, Gas Mark 6) for about 30 minutes, until the filling is set and the pastry golden brown. Garnish with sprigs of parsley.

Mocha meringue flans

INGREDIENTS	METRIC	IMP.	U.S.
Butter	175 g	6 oz	$\frac{3}{4}$ cup
Plain [all-purpose] flour	350 g	12 oz	3 cups
2 eggs			
FILLING			
Plain chocolate	175 g	6 oz	6 squares
2 tspn instant coffee powder			
Double [whipping] cream	300 ml	$\frac{1}{2}$ pint	$1\frac{1}{4}$ cups
Soft [light] brown sugar	100 g	4 oz	$\frac{1}{2}$ cup
2 eggs, separated			
Castor [granulated] sugar	100 g	4 oz	$\frac{1}{2}$ cup

Rub the butter into the flour and combine with the egg. Knead lightly, roll out and use to line two 7 inch/18 cm flan rings on baking sheets. Grate the chocolate, reserve one third for decoration, and mix the remainder with the coffee, cream, brown sugar and egg yolks. Pour in the flan case. Bake in a moderately hot oven (400°F, 200°C, Gas Mark 6) for 15-20 minutes, until set. Whisk the egg whites and sugar until glossy and thick and pipe or fork on top of flans. Return to the oven for a further 5-10 minutes. Chill and serve sprinkled with reserved chocolate.

Orange gingerbread fingers

INGREDIENTS	METRIC	IMP.	U.S.
Treacle [molasses]	110 ml	4 fl oz	$\frac{1}{2}$ cup
2 beaten eggs			
Chopped candied orange peel	50 g	2 oz	$\frac{1}{3}$ cup
Chopped stem ginger	50 g	2 oz	$\frac{1}{3}$ cup
Grated rind and juice of 1 orange			
Castor [granulated] sugar	100 g	4 oz	$\frac{1}{2}$ cup
Plain [all-purpose] flour	350 g	12 oz	3 cups
Pinch salt			
1 tspn bicarbonate of soda [baking soda]			
1 tspn ground cinnamon			
2 tspn ground ginger			
Butter	100 g	4 oz	$\frac{1}{2}$ cup
Little ginger syrup			

Warm the treacle and stir in the eggs, chopped peel, chopped ginger, orange rind and juice and the sugar. Sieve the flour, salt, bicarbonate of soda and the spices into a bowl and rub in the butter. Stir in the treacle mixture and mix well. Add a little ginger syrup if necessary to give a pouring consistency. Transfer the mixture to a lined 9 inch/22 cm square cake tin and bake in a moderate oven (325°F, 170°C, Gas Mark 3) for $1-1\frac{1}{4}$ hours. Serve cut into fingers.

Café Napoléon Dissolve 1 teaspoon sugar in 1 tablespoon brandy in each cup. Strain in hot black coffee to fill, swirl with lightly whipped double (whipping) cream and sprinkle with ground cinnamon.

Chinese party   Serves 6

Chinese-style rice soup
Perfection pork with celery
Buttered noodles
Chinese toffee apples

Chinese-style rice soup

INGREDIENTS	METRIC	IMP.	U.S.
1 tbspn oil			
Long grain rice	100 g	4 oz	$\frac{1}{2}$ cup
Chicken stock [broth]	1.5 litres	3 pints	4 pints
1 carrot			
1 leek, trimmed			
2 stalks celery			
Salt and pepper			

Heat the oil, use to fry the rice for a few minutes, until transparent. Add the stock, bring to the boil and simmer for 30 minutes. Meanwhile finely chop the carrot, leek and celery. Add the chopped vegetables, simmer for a further 5 minutes, and adjust the seasoning.

Perfection pork with celery

INGREDIENTS	METRIC	IMP.	U.S.
Pork fillet [tenderloin]	675 g	1½ lb	1½ lb
Butter	40 g	1½ oz	3 tbspn
Carrots	225 g	8 oz	½ lb
4 stalks celery			
1 tspn salt			
Freshly ground black pepper			
1 tspn cumin powder			
Chicken stock [broth]	450 ml	¾ pint	2 cups
1 tspn cornflour [cornstarch]			

Cut the pork into very thin slices. Sauté in the butter for two minutes. Slice the carrots into julienne strips. Slice the celery stalks diagonally. Add the carrots, celery, seasonings and chicken stock to the pork. Simmer for six minutes or until the vegetables are just tender. Remove the meat and vegetables to a hot serving dish. Mix the cornflour with a little cold water and pour into the hot stock. Simmer until the sauce thickens and clears, stirring constantly. Taste and adjust seasonings. Pour the sauce over the meat and vegetables. Serve with noodles, and a very hotly spiced fruit chutney.

Chinese party
Chinese toffee apples

INGREDIENTS	METRIC	IMP.	U.S.
1 tbspn sesame seeds			
4 eating apples			
1 tbspn cornflour [cornstarch]			
Sugar	100 g	4 oz	½ cup
2 tbspn corn oil			

Spread the sesame seeds on a sheet of foil and toast under a hot grill until golden. Peel, core and cut the apples into small chunks. Toss in cornflour. Dissolve the sugar slowly in the oil until it becomes a thick syrup with a little oil floating on top and pale golden brown in colour. Stir in the sesame seeds. Drop in a few apple chunks at a time, remove with a fork and pile up in a warm serving dish. To serve, turn a spoonful of toffee-coated chunks at a time into a bowl of iced water and immediately remove with a slotted draining spoon on to individual plates.

Fiesta party

Serves 4

Paella
Spanish rice and sausage salad
Sangria

Paella

INGREDIENTS	METRIC	IMP.	U.S.
2 large cooked crab or lobster claws			
1 medium onion			
4 chicken portions			
2 tbspn oil			
Long grain rice	350 g	12 oz	1½ cups
¼ tspn powdered saffron			
Hot chicken stock [broth]	1 litre +	2 pints	5 cups
Freshly-cooked shelled mussels	225 g	8 oz	1 cup
Salt and pepper			

Remove the crab or lobster from the shell. Chop the onion and divide each chicken portion in half. Heat the oil in a large wide shallow pan, add the onion and chicken pieces and fry gently for 15 minutes. Stir in the rice, saffron and stock, bring to the boil, cover and simmer for 10 minutes. Stir the rice mixture, arrange the pieces of crab or lobster, and the mussels in the pan. Season to taste and continue cooking gently for 15-20 minutes, until the rice is tender, and the liquid has been absorbed.

Spanish rice and sausage salad

INGREDIENTS	METRIC	IMP.	U.S.
1 chicken stock [bouillon] cube			
Boiling water	450 ml	¾ pint	2 cups
1 green pepper			
1 large onion			
Butter	50 g	2 oz	¼ cup
Long grain rice	225 g	8 oz	½ lb
¼ tspn ground cinnamon			
¼ tspn powdered saffron			
Salt and ground black pepper			
Chipolata sausages [thin pork links]	450 g	1 lb	1 lb
4 slices fresh pineapple			
Endive [green salad] to garnish			

Dissolve the stock cube in the boiling water. Deseed and slice the pepper and finely slice the onion. Melt the butter and use to fry the pepper and onion slices until softened. Stir in the rice and fry until it begins to turn golden. Add sufficient stock to cover the rice and mix in the spices. Continue cooking slowly, adding more stock as required and stirring frequently, until the rice is cooked. Season to taste with salt and pepper. Meanwhile, grill the sausages and pineapple slices and keep hot. Serve the rice piled up in a warm serving dish with the sausages and pineapple on top. Garnish with green salad.

Sangria is a refreshing wine cup very suitable to serve with these Spanish dishes for a party. Dissolve 225 g/8 oz/1 cup sugar in 300 ml/½ pint/1¼ cups water in a pan. Add a stick of cinnamon or 1 teaspoon ground cinnamon and boil for 5 minutes. Cool. Slice 2 oranges and 2 lemons into a large bowl and pour over the syrup. Leave to stand for 4 hours. Crush about 24 ice cubes, add to the bowl with 1 bottle of red wine and 4 tablespoons of white rum, or any fruit liqueur. Stir well and add about 900 ml/1½ pints/ 4 cups soda water (club soda). Serve in chilled wine glasses.

Curry party
Serves 8

Eggs in curry cream
Fruited lamb curry
Fluffy boiled rice
Canned lychees with vanilla ice cream

Eggs in curry cream

INGREDIENTS	METRIC	IMP.	U.S.
8 eggs			
2 large onions, sliced			
Lard	50 g	2 oz	$\frac{1}{4}$ cup
2 tbspn curry powder			
1 tbspn flour			
1 large cooking [baking] apple			
Stock	600 ml	1 pint	$2\frac{1}{2}$ cups
1 tbspn chutney			
1 tbspn brown sugar			
1 tbspn marmalade			
Juice of $\frac{1}{2}$ lemon			
Salt			
4 tbspn evaporated milk			
Long grain rice	225 g	8 oz	$\frac{1}{2}$ lb

Hard-boil the eggs, shell them and place in a basin. Cover with hot water. Fry the onions gently in the lard for 10 minutes until soft. Stir in the curry powder and flour and cook gently for 2 minutes. Peel, core and chop the apple, add to the pan and cook for 3 minutes. Gradually add the stock and bring to the boil, stirring constantly. Add the chutney, brown sugar, marmalade and lemon juice to the sauce. Taste and add salt. Simmer for 25 to 30 minutes, stirring occasionally. Strain the sauce into a clean saucepan, add the evaporated milk and bring to boiling point. Meanwhile cook the rice in boiling salted water for about 12 minutes. Strain and spread on a hot serving dish. Dry the eggs, cut in half lengthwise and arrange on top of the rice. Spoon over the hot sauce.

Fruited lamb curry

INGREDIENTS	METRIC	IMP.	U.S.
Boned leg or shoulder of lamb	575 g	1¼ lb	1¼ lb
2 tbspn flour			
Salt and pepper			
1 medium onion			
1 tbspn oil			
1 tbspn curry powder			
2 tspn curry paste			
Stock or water	450 ml	¾ pint	2 cups
1 apple			
1 tbspn sultanas [golden raisins]			
Dried apricots	50 g	2 oz	⅓ cup
2 tbspn lemon juice			

Trim excess fat from lamb and dice. Turn in flour seasoned with salt and pepper. Chop the onion. Fry the lamb and onion in the oil until well browned. Stir in the curry powder and curry paste and cook for 2-3 minutes. Gradually stir in the stock or water. Bring to the boil and simmer for 10 minutes. Peel and chop the apple and add to the meat. Stir in the sultanas, apricots and lemon juice. Cover and simmer for one hour or until the meat is tender. Serve with plain boiled rice and a variety of accompaniments: onion rings, sliced tomatoes, desiccated coconut, peanuts, sliced bananas and poppadoms.

Pasta party Serves 6

Party pasta with mussels
Tuna tetrazzini
Green lasagne with beef
Italian baked peaches

Party pasta with mussels

INGREDIENTS	METRIC	IMP.	U.S.
Fresh mussels	2.5 litres	4 pints	3 quarts
Dry white wine	225 ml	8 fl oz	1 cup
2 tbspn chopped parsley			
1 tbspn chopped shallots or onion			
Pasta shells	225 g	8 oz	2 cups
Butter	50 g	2 oz	¼ cup
Grated rind of ½ lemon			
¼ tspn freshly ground black pepper			
Chopped tomatoes	225 g	8 oz	1 cup
Salt and pepper			
Single cream [half & half]	50 ml	2 fl oz	¼ cup
Lemon juice			

Scrub the mussel shells and scrape off the 'beards'. Place in a large saucepan with the wine, one tablespoon of the chopped parsley and the shallots. Cover and simmer over low heat until they open, about 15 minutes. Discard any which remain closed. Remove the mussels and pull the top shells off. Meanwhile, cook the pasta shells in boiling salted water for 8-10 minutes or until just tender. Drain and toss with the butter, lemon rind and black pepper. Turn into a serving dish and arrange the mussels in the half shells over the pasta. Cover and keep hot. Add the tomatoes to the wine liquid. Season with salt and pepper. Boil for 5 minutes. Remove from the heat and stir in the cream. Add lemon juice to taste. Pour the sauce over the mussels and pasta. Garnish with the remaining chopped parsley.

76

Tuna tetrazzini

INGREDIENTS	METRIC	IMP.	U.S.
1 small onion			
2 stalks celery			
Butter	40 g	1½ oz	3 tbspns
2 tbspn flour			
½ tspn salt and pinch pepper			
¼ tspn Worcestershire sauce			
Milk	300 ml	½ pint	1¼ cups
Spaghetti	100 g	4 oz	¼ lb
Mushrooms	125 g	4 oz	1 cup
Canned tuna fish	184 g	6½ oz	7 oz
2 tbspn sliced green olives			

Chop the onion and celery finely and sauté in 1 oz/25 g of the butter until soft. Stir in the flour, seasonings and Worcestershire sauce. Cook for 2-3 minutes. Gradually add the milk, stirring until thickened. Cook the spaghetti in boiling salted water until tender. Drain well and mix with the sauce. Slice the mushrooms and fry in the remaining butter. Drain the tuna fish. Alternate layers of the spaghetti mixture, tuna and mushrooms in a lightly greased 2 pint/ generous 1 litre/1½ quart casserole, ending with a layer of spaghetti. Sprinkle with Parmesan cheese and place sliced olives on top. Bake in a moderate oven (350°F, 180°C, Gas Mark 4) for 30 minutes.

Green lasagne with beef

INGREDIENTS	METRIC	IMP.	U.S.
Green lasagne	225 g	8 oz	½ lb
1 tbspn oil			
SAUCE			
1 large onion			
1 large carrot			
1 large green sweet pepper			
1 clove garlic			
Streaky [side] bacon slices	100 g	4 oz	¼ lb
Butter	25 g	1 oz	2 tbspn
Minced [ground] beef	450 g	1 lb	1 lb
Canned tomatoes	400 g	14 oz	14 oz
2 tbspn tomato purée [paste]			
½ tspn dried mixed herbs			
Beef stock [broth]	150 ml	¼ pint	⅔ cup
½ tspn sugar			

First make the sauce. Chop the onion and carrot, deseed and chop the green pepper, crush the garlic and derind and chop the bacon. Melt the butter and use to fry the onion, carrot, green pepper, garlic, bacon and minced beef until lightly browned. Add the tomatoes, tomato purée, herbs, stock, sugar and a little seasoning. Stir well, bring to the boil and cook for 30 minutes. Adjust the seasoning. Meanwhile break each strip of lasagne in half then cook in boiling salted water for about 10 minutes, until just tender. Drain well and toss lightly with the oil over low heat to separate. Keep hot. Arrange a bed of cooked lasagne in a shallow serving dish and pour the meat into the centre.

Italian baked peaches

INGREDIENTS	METRIC	IMP.	U.S.
6 large peaches			
Butter	15 g	½ oz	1 tbspn
Castor [granulated] sugar	25 g	1 oz	¼ cup
1 egg yolk			
Crushed macaroons	50 g	2 oz	½ cup
1 tbspn ground almonds			
Pinch ground cinnamon			

Peel, halve and stone the peaches. Place, cut side up, in a buttered ovenproof dish. Combine all the other ingredients. Divide between the peaches, mounding up slightly. Bake in a moderate oven (350°F, 180°C, Gas Mark 4) for about 25 minutes.

Time-saver pasta party Serves 12

Turkey and noodle casserole
Pasta shells with bolognese sauce
Turkey and artichoke savoury
Bunches of white and black grapes

Turkey and noodle casserole

INGREDIENTS	METRIC	IMP.	U.S.
Butter	75 g	3 oz	6 tbspns
Flour	25 g	1 oz	5 tbspns
Turkey stock	600 ml	1 pint	2½ cups
Single cream [half & half]	300 ml	½ pint	1¼ cups
6 tspn dry white wine	6 tbspns	6 tbspns	½ cup
Grated Parmesan cheese	75 g	3 oz	¾ cup
Sliced mushrooms	350 g	12 oz	3 cups
Noodles	225 g	8 oz	½ lb
Cooked turkey meat, chopped	1 kg	2 lb	4 cups
Salt and pepper			
Parsley sprigs			

Melt 1 oz/25 g/2 tablespoons of the butter in a pan and stir in the flour. Cook for 2-3 minutes, stirring, to prevent the flour from becoming brown. Gradually stir in the stock. Bring to the boil over a moderate heat, stirring until thickened. Stir in the cream and wine and reheat, but do not allow to boil. Stir in 2 oz/50 g/½ cup of the cheese. Melt the remaining butter in a frying pan and sauté the mushrooms until lightly browned. Cook the noodles in a pan of boiling, salted water until just tender. Drain well.

In a large casserole, place two-thirds of the sauce and the mushrooms, the noodles and turkey, in layers. Add salt and pepper to taste and top with the remaining sauce and mushrooms. Sprinkle over the reserved grated cheese, place in a moderately hot oven (375°F, 190°C, Gas Mark 5) for 15 minutes until browned. Top with parsley sprigs.

Pasta shells with bolognese sauce

INGREDIENTS	METRIC	IMP.	U.S.
Pasta shells	225 g	8 oz	2 cup
Diced cooked turkey	350 g	12 oz	2 cups
Chicken stock [broth]	150 ml	¼ pint	½ cup
Canned Bolognese sauce	289 g	10 oz	10 oz
2 tbspn blanched almonds			
Little butter			

Cook the pasta shells in plenty of boiling salted water for about 15 minutes until tender. Drain well. Meanwhile, reheat the turkey in the stock, heat the Bolognese sauce in a separate pan and fry the almonds lightly in a little butter until golden. Place the pasta in a greased ovenproof dish, top with the turkey, spoon over the sauce and scatter over the almonds.

Quick tip for pasta dishes Use cooked chicken or turkey as the basic ingredient for all these big hearty dishes. The two meats are interchangeable. Canned bolognese sauce saves cooking too and there are other canned pasta sauces to choose from.

Turkey and artichoke savoury

INGREDIENTS	METRIC	IMP.	U.S.
Butter	25 g	1 oz	2 tbspn
Sliced mushrooms	100 g	4 oz	1 cup
Flour	15 g	½ oz	2 tbspn
Turkey stock	150 ml	¼ pint	⅔ cup
Sherry	2 tbspn	2 tbspn	3 tbspn
Pinch dried rosemary			
Salt and pepper			
½ tspn paprika pepper			
Cooked turkey meat,	450 g	1 lb	1 lb
Canned artichoke hearts, drained	450 g	1 lb	1 lb
Cooked spaghetti	450 g	1 lb	1 lb

Melt the butter in a pan and sauté the mushrooms until lightly browned. Sprinkle in the flour and cook for a further 1-2 minutes, stirring. Gradually add the stock and sherry, stirring. Add the rosemary and seasoning. Chop the turkey, place with artichoke hearts in a casserole and pour over the mushroom mixture. Place in a moderately hot oven (375°F, 190°C, Gas Mark 5) for about 15 minutes, adding a little extra stock if necessary. Serve with cooked spaghetti.

Pizza party Serves 8

Tray pizza
Mediterranean deep pizza

Basic quick pizza dough

INGREDIENTS	METRIC	IMP.	U.S.
2 (283 g/10 oz) sachets white bread mix			
Hot water	400 ml	14 fl oz	1¾ cups

Place the bread mix in a bowl and add the water which should be as hot as the hand can stand. Beat with a wooden spoon or by hand until a dough is formed then turn out on a floured surface and knead for 5 minutes. Divide the dough into two portions, one slightly larger than the other. Use the larger portion to make a Tray pizza and the smaller one to make a Mediterranean deep pizza.

Tray pizza

INGREDIENTS	METRIC	IMP.	U.S.
The larger portion of pizza dough			
Canned anchovy fillets	*100 g*	*4 oz*	*4oz*
1 medium onion			
2 cans tomatoes, each	*396 g*	*14 oz*	*14 oz*
Mushrooms	*50 g*	*2 oz*	*2 oz*
2 tbspn tomato purée [paste]			
1 tspn dried mixed herbs			
Salt and pepper			
Grated strong Cheddar cheese	*50 g*	*2 oz*	*½ cup*
1 tbspn grated Parmesan cheese			
Black olives	*50 g*	*2 oz*	*⅓ cup*

Roll out the dough and use to line a greased tin measuring 18 cm/7 inches by 28 cm/11 inches. Allow to rise in a warm place until double in bulk. Drain the oil from the anchovies into a pan. Thinly slice the onion, add to the oil and cook until limp. Drain the tomatoes and chop the mushrooms. Add to the pan with the tomato purée and herbs. Stir well and roughly chop the tomatoes. Add 2 tablespoons liquid from the cans of tomatoes and cook gently until the mixture is thick. Season well with salt and pepper. Spread over the dough to within 1 cm/½ inch of the edges and sprinkle the cheeses over the top. Bake in a moderately hot oven (400°F, 200°C, Gas Mark 6) for about 20 minutes, until risen and just golden round the edges. Cut the anchovy fillets in half lengthways and arrange in a lattice pattern over the top of the pizza. Put the olives evenly in the spaces and return the pizza to the oven for 5 minutes.

Mediterranean deep pizza

INGREDIENTS	METRIC	IMP.	U.S.
The smaller portion of pizza dough			
1 medium onion			
Little olive oil			
Canned tuna	*100 g*	*4 oz*	*4 oz*
Canned red pimientoes	*85 g*	*3¾ oz*	*3¾ oz*
Peeled prawns [large shrimp]	*75 g*	*3 oz*	*3 oz*
Canned dressed crab	*45 g*	*1¼ oz*	*1¼ oz*
Pepper			
Grated Cheddar cheese	*75 g*	*3 oz*	*¾ cup*
Chopped parsley			

Roll out the dough and use to line an 18 cm/7½ inch shallow cake tin. Allow to rise in a warm place until double in bulk. Finely chop the onion and fry in a little olive oil until soft. Drain well. Drain and flake the tuna. Drain the pimientoes, chop them and add 2 tablespoons of the liquid from the can. Combine the onion, pimiento mixture, tuna, prawns, crabmeat and pepper to taste. Brush the pizza base with oil, top with the pimiento and seafood mixture and sprinkle with the cheese, parsley and a little extra oil. Bake in a hot oven (425°F, 220°C, Gas Mark 7) for about 30 minutes.

Engagement party

Serves 8

Avocado cheese flan
Crunchy crisp dip with crackers
Sweetheart gâteau
Meringue gâteau
Marrons glacés

Sweetheart gâteau

INGREDIENTS	METRIC	IMP.	U.S.
Plain [all-purpose] flour	150 g	5 oz	1¼ cups
1 tspn baking powder			
1 tbspn cocoa [unsweetened cocoa powder]			
Castor [granulated] sugar	350 g	12 oz	1½ cups
Soft margarine	175 g	6 oz	¾ cup
3 eggs			
4 tbspn water			
White chocolate bars	75 g	3 oz	3 oz
'Philly' soft cheese	175 g	6 oz	6 oz
2 tbspn golden [corn] syrup			
Drained canned mandarin segments	225 g	8 oz	1 cup

Sift the flour, baking powder and cocoa into a mixing bowl. Add half the sugar, the margarine and eggs. Beat with a wooden spoon for 1-2 minutes, until the mixture is smooth and soft. Divide between two greased and lined 20 cm/ 8 inch shallow cake tins. Bake in a moderate oven (350°F, 180°C, Gas Mark 4) for 20-25 minutes, until firm to the touch. Cool on a wire rack. Cut a circle of greaseproof paper the size of one cake tin, fold in half and cut out half a heart shape. Unfold to give a complete heart shape. Place pattern on each cake and cut to heart shape. Place the remaining sugar in a pan with the water and heat gently to dissolve. Boil without stirring until the caramel is a rich golden brown. Pour immediately on to a baking sheet lined with greased greaseproof paper. Tilt to form an even layer of caramel and allow to cool. Melt the chocolate in a basin over a pan of hot water. Cream the 'Philly' with the syrup until smooth, then beat in the chocolate. Chop half the mandarins and mix with 2 tablespoons of the chocolate mixture. Use to sandwich the heart-shaped cakes together. Remove the caramel from the paper and break into small pieces. Spread the sides of the cake with a little more of the chocolate mixture and roll in caramel chippings. Decorate the top of the cake with the remainder of the chocolate mixture, mandarins and caramel.

Marrons glacés

INGREDIENTS	METRIC	IMP.	U.S.
Large chestnuts	1 kg	2 lb	2 lb
2 tspn vanilla essence [extract]			
Sugar	450 g	1 lb	2 cups
Water	300 ml	½ pint	1¼ cups
Pinch cream of tartar			
SECOND SYRUP			
Sugar	450 g	1 lb	2 cups
Water	150 ml	¼ pint	½ cup +
1 tspn vanilla essence [extract]			

Slit the shells and boil the chestnuts for 5 minutes only. Skin, cook until tender in sufficient water to cover, flavoured with the vanilla essence. Make a syrup with the sugar, water and cream of tartar. Boil to the thread stage (225°F, 119°C). Add the chestnuts and boil for 1 minute. Remove from the heat, leave chestnuts to soak for 24 hours, drain. Make the second syrup with the sugar, water and vanilla essence. Boil to the firm ball stage (250°F, 126°C). Add the chestnuts, coat well with the syrup, remove and space out to dry on foil. Wrap individually in foil.
Note: The remaining syrups need not be wasted. Combine them, heat slowly and re-dissolve, add a small knob of butter and 2 tablespoons rum. Peel and slice 4 bananas lengthwise, arrange in a buttered shallow ovenproof dish, pour over the rum syrup and bake in a hot oven (425°F, 220°C, Gas Mark 7) for 10 minutes.

Crunchy crisp dip

INGREDIENTS	METRIC	IMP.	U.S.
Cream cheese	75 g	3 oz	3 oz
2 tspn ketchup [catsup]			
1 tspn made mustard			
Pinch ground ginger			
Crumbled cooked bacon	50 g	2 oz	½ cup
Soured cream	5 tbspn	5 tbspn	⅓ cup

Soften the cream cheese. Beat in the remaining ingredients until well blended. Refrigerate for 1 hour to blend flavours. Serve with potato crisps and small savoury crackers.

Avocado cheese flan

INGREDIENTS	METRIC	IMP.	U.S.
Plain [all-purpose] flour	150 g	6 oz	1½ cups
Margarine	50 g	2 oz	¼ cup
Lard	50 g	2 oz	¼ cup
1 egg yolk			
1 tbspn cold water			
FILLING			
1 onion			
2 beaten eggs			
Grated Cheddar cheese	125 g	4 oz	1 cup
3 tbspn milk			
2 medium avocados			
Salt and pepper			
2 sliced tomatoes			

Sieve the flour into a bowl and rub in the fats. Bind with the egg yolk and water and chill the pastry well. Roll out and use to line an 8 inch/20 cm flan dish. Finely chop the onion and mix with the eggs, cheese and milk in a large bowl. Halve the avocados, remove the stones and dice the flesh. Stir avocado into the egg mixture and add seasoning to taste. Pour the mixture into the pastry case and top with the tomato slices. Cook in a moderately hot oven (375°F, 190°C, Gas Mark 5) for 30 minutes. Serve hot or cold.

Meringue gâteau

INGREDIENTS	METRIC	IMP.	U.S.
4 egg whites			
Castor [granulated] sugar	225 g	8 oz	1 cup
2 tbspn toasted flaked [slivered] almonds			
FILLING			
Granulated sugar	50 g	2 oz	¼ cup
4 tbspn water			
2 egg yolks			
Plain [unsweetened] chocolate	50 g	2 oz	2 squares
Unsalted butter	175 g	6 oz	¾ cup

Left: Separate the eggs. Whisk the whites until stiff.
Centre: When the 3 baking sheets have been lined with non-stick parchment, draw round the loose base of a 20 cm/ 8 inch cake tin to produce the required circles on the parchment.
Right: The last of the three meringue layers is sprinkled with toasted flaked almonds.

Place the egg whites in a large bowl. Whisk them until stiff then gradually whisk in the castor sugar until the mixture is thick and glossy. Line 3 baking sheets with non-stick cooking parchment and draw a 20 cm/8 inch circle on each one. Spread the meringue mixture into the three circles. Sprinkle the top of one meringue round with the almonds. Bake them in a cool oven (300°F, 150°C, Gas Mark 2) for about 1 hour. Cool, then strip off the Bakewell parchment. To make the filling, place the sugar and water together in a pan and heat gently until the sugar has dissolved. Boil steadily until the syrup reaches a temperature of 216°F/100°C. (To test without a thermometer, cool a little syrup in a spoon, press a drop between finger and thumb then open them. The syrup should form a thin thread.) When the bubbles have disappeared, pour the syrup on to the egg yolks and whisk steadily until the mixture is like a thick mousse. Melt the chocolate in a basin over a pan of hot water. Cream the butter then gradually beat in the egg mousse and the melted chocolate. Beat until the filling is cool and thick enough to hold its shape then sandwich the meringue layers together, placing the almond layer on top.

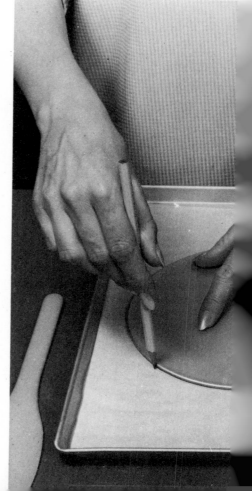

Bread, soup and cheese party Serves 8

Sandwich loaf
Cottage loaf
Pizzas with mozzarella
Winter vegetable minestra

Sausage and bean soup
Cheddar cheese platter
with radishes

Basic white bread

INGREDIENTS	METRIC	IMP.	U.S.
2 tspn sugar			
Warm water	300 ml	$\frac{1}{2}$ pint	$1\frac{1}{4}$ cups
Dried yeast or	25 g	1 oz	$2\frac{1}{2}$ tbspn
Fresh [compressed] yeast	50 g	2 oz	1 cake
Margarine	75 g	3 oz	$\frac{1}{3}$ cup
Hot water	600 ml	1 pint	$2\frac{1}{2}$ cups
1 tbspn salt			
Strong plain [all-purpose] flour	1.4 kg	3 lb	12 cups

Pizzas with mozzarella

INGREDIENTS	METRIC	IMP.	U.S.
Tomatoes	450 g	1 lb	1 lb
Mozzarella cheese	225 g	8 oz	$\frac{1}{2}$ lb
1 tspn dried oregano			
Salt and pepper			
3 tbspn olive oil			

Dissolve the sugar in the warm water and sprinkle in the yeast. Leave in a warm place until frothy, about 10 minutes. Melt the margarine in the hot water, stir in the salt and cool to lukewarm. Add a little of the flour and beat for 2 minutes. Add the yeast liquid and sufficient flour to make a stiff dough. Turn out on a lightly floured board and knead until the dough is smooth and elastic, about 10 minutes. Shape the dough into a ball and place in a greased bowl. Cover with a damp cloth (or slip it into a greased polythene bag) and let it rise in a warm place until doubled in bulk, about one hour. Turn out and knead lightly. Divide into three.

Sandwich loaf: Shape one third of the dough into a loaf and place in a greased 2 lb/1 kg loaf tin. Cover and let rise until double in bulk, about 40 minutes. Bake in a hot oven (425°F, 220°C, Gas Mark 7) for 10 minutes, then bake in a moderately hot oven (375°F, 190°C, Gas Mark 5) for 40 minutes or until the loaf sounds hollow when tapped. Turn out immediately and let cool on a wire rack.

Cottage loaf: Shape another portion of the dough into one large ball and one smaller ball. Place the large ball on a greased baking tray and place the smaller ball on top. Push the handle of a wooden spoon through the centre of the dough, through to the baking tray. Let the cottage loaf rise in a warm place until doubled in bulk. Follow the baking directions above.

Use the remaining dough to make pizzas. Roll to $\frac{1}{4}$ inch/6 mm thickness. Cut the dough into 8 circles and place on greased baking trays. Slice the tomatoes and Mozzarella cheese thinly. Cover each dough circle with a layer of tomatoes and cheese. Sprinkle with oregano, salt and pepper. Add another layer of tomatoes and cheese and brush the oil over each pizza. Bake in a moderately hot oven (400°F, 200°C, Gas Mark 6) for 25-30 minutes.

Winter vegetable minestra

INGREDIENTS	METRIC	IMP.	U.S.
1 medium carrot			
1 large onion			
1 small parsnip			
1 small turnip			
2 tbspn oil			
Beef stock [broth]	600 ml	1 pint	2½ cups
1 bay leaf			
½ tspn salt			
¼ tspn pepper			
1 small potato			
Canned tomatoes	227 g	8 oz	1 cup
1 tspn dried parsley			
Vermicelli noodles	25 g	1 oz	¼ cup
Parmesan cheese			

Peel and cut the carrot, onion, parsnip and turnip into narrow strips. Heat the oil in a saucepan and fry the vegetables until limp, about 5 minutes. Add the beef stock, bay leaf, salt and pepper. Simmer for 30 minutes. Peel and cut the potato into narrow strips. Add potato strips to the vegetable-stock mixture and simmer for a further 20 minutes. Stir in the tomatoes, parsley and vermicelli. Simmer 10 minutes, pour into hot soup bowls and sprinkle with grated Parmesan cheese.

Sausage and bean soup

INGREDIENTS	METRIC	IMP.	U.S.
Dried red kidney beans	100 g	4 oz	½ cup
Shredded cabbage	175 g	6 oz	2 cups
2 medium potatoes			
2 medium onions			
1 large leek			
2 medium carrots			
Chicken stock [broth]	900 ml	1½ pints	3¾ cups
Pork chipolata sausages [small pork links]	450 g	1 lb	1 lb

Soak the beans in cold water to cover overnight. Drain, place in a large pan. Slice the potatoes, onions and leek and chop the carrots. Add these to the pan with the stock and seasoning. Bring to the boil, stir well, cover and simmer for 2 hours. Twist each sausage into three, to give chains of three small sausages. Add to the soup with the cabbage and simmer for a further 15 minutes. Adjust the seasoning if necessary.

Toasted cheese party
Serves 6

Anchovy rarebits
Double-crust cinnamon apple pie

Anchovy rarebits

INGREDIENTS	METRIC	IMP.	U.S.
Canned anchovy fillets	50 g	2 oz	2 oz
Milk, about	300 ml	½ pint	1¼ cups
4 tbspn Guinness			
Butter	40 g	1½ oz	3 tbspn
Flour	40 g	1½ oz	⅓ cup
Grated mature Cheddar cheese	225 g	8 oz	2 cups
Pinch pepper			
6 large slices buttered toast			
Few sprigs of parsley and tomato wedges			

Drain the anchovies well and dry them on soft kitchen paper. Reserve six for the garnish and halve each one of these lengthways. Chop the remaining anchovies. Take 4 tablespoons milk from the measured quantity and replace with the Guinness. Melt the butter in a pan and stir in the flour. Cook for 1 minute then remove from the heat and gradually add the milk mixture. Bring to the boil, stirring constantly, then cook for 1 minute. Remove from the heat, add the chopped anchovies, three quarters of the cheese and the pepper. Stir over gentle heat until the cheese has melted. Spread the rarebit mixture on the buttered toast, and cut each slice into two triangles. Top each piece with a strip of anchovy, sprinkle with a little cheese and a drop or two of anchovy oil. Grill for about 2 minutes, until the cheese has melted. Arrange on a serving plate and garnish with parsley sprigs and tomato wedges.

Variations on rarebit For a large party, add different finishes to the rarebit mixture, omitting the anchovies:
Sprinkle a teaspoon of drained capers over the cheese mixture before putting under the grill.
Sprinkle fried bacon dice on the finished rarebits.
Place a slice of thin, lean ham under the rarebit mixture.
Top the finished rarebits with fried onion rings.
Stir some finely chopped smoked salmon pieces into the rarebit mixture.

Double-crust cinnamon apple pie

INGREDIENTS	METRIC	IMP.	U.S.
Butter	50 g	2 oz	½ cup
3 egg yolks			
1 tbspn water			
Plain [all-purpose] flour	225 g	8 oz	2 cups
Castor [granulated] sugar	50 g	2 oz	¼ cup
½ tspn vanilla essence [extract]			
Little milk			
FILLING			
2 large cooking [baking] apples			
2 tspn lemon juice			
4 tbspn water			
½ tspn ground cinnamon			
2 tbspn soft brown sugar			
2 tbspn granulated sugar			
1 tspn grated lemon rind			

First make the pastry. Dice the butter and lightly beat the egg yolks with the water. Sift the flour on to a pastry board, make a well in the centre and place the butter, sugar, vanilla and egg mixture in it. Using the fingertips, gradually draw in the flour and blend it with the mixture. Knead lightly until smooth, form into a ball and chill while you make the filling. Peel and core the apples. Slice thinly and cook with the lemon juice and water until soft. Add the spice, sugars and lemon rind. Cook, stirring, until the sugar has dissolved. Remove from the heat and beat until smooth. Cool. Roll out the pastry thinly. Use rather more than half to line an 8 inch/ 20 cm flan tin. Fill with the cooked apple mixture and use the remaining pastry to cover the top. Dampen the edges and seal well together. Cut a steam vent and use pastry trimmings to decorate the pie. Brush with milk and bake in a hot oven (425°F, 220°C, Gas Mark 7) for 15 minutes, then reduce heat slightly and bake for a further 20 minutes, or until the pastry is golden brown.

Adding inspiration to fruit

When a hot pudding or cold dessert does not figure on the dinner menu, fruit makes a welcome change. In most homes the fruit bowl contains a selection of apples, bananas and oranges, replenished once a week. But that isn't nearly the end of the possible selection, so when less familiar fruits are around, give them a trial. Fruit can be offered in various ways; whole, prepared raw, or cooked.

Fresh from the fruit bowl

Follow a few simple rules to make sure it is always in peak condition. Wash all fruit you buy that is to be eaten raw before putting it into the bowl, pat dry with soft kitchen paper and polish hard fruits such as apples and pears with a soft clean cloth. This gives you an opportunity to note any extra-ripe fruit or damaged specimens that need eating up quickly. Discard any over-ripe grapes from a bunch. Make sure you get a whole bunch, as the salesman may put several small ones and a few loose grapes together; or, if this is what you bring home, sort out and set aside the loose ones and small bunches for a fruit salad. The same rule applies to bananas; if the skins are getting freckled and really golden, they are useful for slicing because any brown parts can be discarded. Although under-ripe bananas are rather flavourless, there is only a short period when they are just perfect. Stocking up the fruit bowl for a week ought to provide enough less-than-perfect specimens to make the basis for one lovely fresh fruit salad. You have two ways to round this out: Peel and slice the fruit according to its kind and combine with the contents of a small can of fruit; peach slices, pineapple pieces or apricot halves are ideal for the purpose. Or, if you have enough fresh fruit, make your own syrup. Dissolve 4 tablespoons sugar in 8 tablespoons of water over low heat, allow to bubble away gently for a couple of minutes, then add 1 tablespoon lemon juice and stir well. Cool and when the syrup is quite cold pour over the fruit. Double the quantities if necessary. Do not peel or slice fruits which discolour quickly such as peaches and pears, until the syrup is ready for them. Remember that grapes are much nicer peeled, halved and pipped for salads, unless you can find the

small seedless white grapes which are perfect as they are. Red fruits including strawberries, raspberries and currants should be added at serving time as they colour the syrup and get soggy if kept waiting.

Vary the selection of fruit in your bowl as much as possible so that the family always finds it interesting. To the constant friends, apples, bananas and oranges add in their season the following: apricots, cherries, clementines, fresh dates, pink grapefruits, grapes, greengages, kiwifruits, lychees, mangoes, nectarines, passion fruit, pawpaws, peaches, pears, pineapple, plums, pomegranates and satsumas.

Special occasion fruit bowl

A rather stylised arrangement in the Victorian manner makes a lovely table centrepiece, and nothing is more effective than a pyramid built up round a small pineapple. Choose one with fresh green spiky leaves for the best effect. Pieces of fruit can usually be arranged to support each other but glossy green leaves can be introduced – large variegated ivy or other evergreens will do very well. Green tissue paper, easily bought at Christmas time, may be helpful too. During some periods of the year the choice of fruit is

limited. A pretty bowl can be arranged with contrasting apples, red and green-skinned, or golden and faintly striped apples. For a party, bunches of black, purplish red and white grapes are easy to arrange, and flower heads can be starred over the arrangement. (Daisy and chrysanthemum heads are easy to hold in place, but if other flower stems are wired with short lengths of florist's wire, there is no problem.) Here are a few suggestions:

Green Granny Smith and Golden Delicious apples dotted with golden-centred white marguerites . . . yellow, red and purple plums grouped round an Israeli Galia melon . . . William pears arranged round a shallow basket piled with mixed nuts. Shelled nuts mixed with raisins can be put on the table with fresh fruit. The combination is splendid. While nuts are in season in their shells, keep a few well-shaped ones and spray with gold, silver or white paint. They are good standbys for decorative arrangements at other times of the year.

Melons are not put in the fruit bowl so often, because they are too large for one person, and need to be prepared for service in the kitchen. Small ones (Ogen, Charentais, Galia) and even miniature Honeydews, can be served as a starter or dessert, sliced across the centre and emptied of pith and pips. Each melon serves two. If ripe enough they need no sugar, but for special occasions it is nice to fill the centre with sweet sherry, port or a fruit liqueur mixed with an appropriate fruit – Cointreau with orange slices, Kirsch with cherries. Large melons cut in slices look lovely, but add an exotic touch occasionally with

sliced ginger from a jar and a trickle of the syrup. To make portions easy to remove, slice the flesh away from the skin using a curved grapefruit knife, then slash across at 2.5 cm/1 inch intervals. Watermelon gives a brilliant splash of colour when available.

Grapefruits also lend themselves to pretty presentation. Slice in half across, loosen the segments with the same curved knife. Cut out the pithy centre and pop in a maraschino cherry (much nicer that a candied one), or spread the flesh with a mixture of rum and brown sugar and slip under the grill to glaze. If you prepare the fruit some time in advance, to serve plain or to be sprinkled with sugar at table, cover the cut surfaces with cling wrap to prevent them from drying out. Just strip off the covering at the last moment.

Fruit compôtes

A fruit compôte is really a salad made of cooked fruit, either fresh, or dried and soaked. Prunes soaked in tea then lightly cooked, dried apple rings and peaches or apricots also pre-soaked in orange juice and gently stewed make good compôtes. Many firm-fleshed fruit such as apricots and plums and also rhubarb are too hard to eat raw even when soaked in fruit-flavoured syrup. Make up the syrup, slice and stone the fruit if needed, or cut the rhubarb stems up finely, and cook in the syrup until just tender. The fruit will not go mushy if cooked this way. Combinations of red fruits such as currants and raspberries are delicious, but add the softer fruit, in this case the raspberries, towards the end of cooking time. Allow the compôte to cool completely, when it will thicken slightly, taste and add an extra touch if desired. Pears could have a drop or two of food colouring added to the syrup to make them more appetising in appearance, and a sprinkling of cinnamon or nutmeg appeals to some tastes.

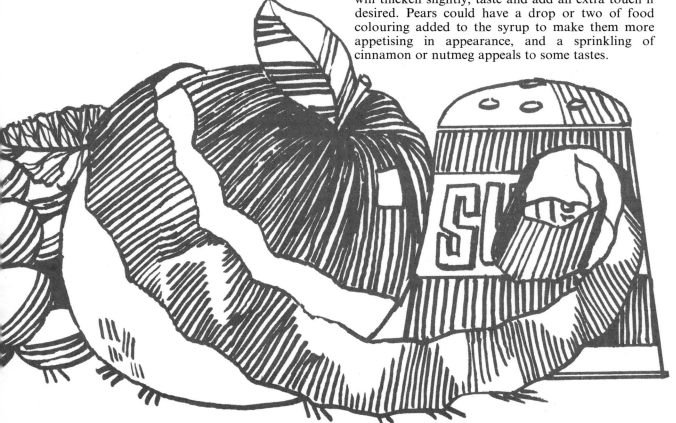

Acknowledgments
The author and publishers thank the following for their help
in supplying photographs for this book, some of which
were adapted from Four Seasons Cookery:
The Sherry Shippers Association, p. 16-17
The Home Baking Bureau, p. 18-19, p. 80-82
Buxted Brand Products by Ross Poultry Ltd., p. 20-21
Bakewell Non-Stick Cooking Parchment, p. 22-25
Kellogg's Kitchen, p. 22-25
Butterball Turkeys, p. 26-27
Kraft Foods Ltd., p. 26-27, p. 83-85
Henkell Trocken, p. 28-33
The Wines from Germany Information Service, p. 28-33
British Turkey Federation, p. 34-43
Mazola Pure Corn Oil, p. 34-43, p. 70-72
The National Dried Fruit Trade Association, p. 34-43
Pyrex and Eve 'glass' by A. Jobling Ltd., p. 34-43
James Robertson & Sons (Preserve Manufacturers) Ltd.,
    p. 34-43
The Tupperware Company, p. 44-45
British Bacon Bureau, p. 49
Pointerware (U.K.) Ltd., p. 48-51
British Sausage Bureau, p. 52-53, p. 73, p. 86-87
John West Foods, p. 56-59, p. 62-63
National Dairy Council, p. 56-59
Birds Eye Foods, p. 60-61
African Groundnut Council, p. 66-67
The U.S. Rice Council, p. 70-72
Hassy Perfection Celery, p. 70-72
Carnation Milk Bureau, p. 74-75
New Zealand Lamb Information Bureau, p. 74-75
Pasta Information Centre, p. 76-77
Princes-Buitoni, p. 78-79
Arthur Guinness, Son & Co., p. 88-89

92

Party MENUS

Index

American griddlecakes 67
Anchovy rarebits 89
Avocado cheese flan 83
Avocado cream 46
Baked egg custard 21
Baked layered pancakes 66
Banana candles 63
Barbecue grilled sandwiches 48
Beat 'n bake Christmas cake 38
Bow ties 62
Brandied mincemeat 38
Caernarvon salad 52
Café Napoléon 69
Cardamom coffee 59
Cart-wheel bananas 51
Cervelat salad 47
Cheddar mushroom caps 56
Cheesey frankfurters 50
Cheesey jacket potatoes 52
Chicken and pimiento aspic mould 33
Chicken fingers in batter 28
Chicken liver pâté pinwheels 30
Chilli barbecue sauce 49
Chinese style rice soup 70
Chinese toffee apples 72
Chocolate challenger 60
Chocolate slim shake 60
Chocolate Viennese torte 58
Cinnamon honey butter 66
Coconut macaroons 18
Cola fancy 60
Consommé starters 35
Cottage cheese pancakes 65
Cottage loaf 86
Crab and sweetcorn pancakes 64
Cranberry orange sauce 35
Cream cheese and herb ribbon
  sandwiches 30
Creamed prawn vol-au-vents 54
Creamy Dijon dip 33
Crunchy crisp dip 83
Curried cheese dip 16
Devon cup 60
Doonside Valentine cake 19
Double-crust cinnamon apple pie 89
Duck biscuits 22
Easter bonnet cake 25
Easter nest cake 25
Easter turkey with potato nests 20
Eggs in curry cream 74
Family fruit cup 60
Festive stuffed eggs 30
Filled celery sticks 44

Florida flip 60
Fondant icing 29
French onion and leek flan 68
Fresh herb scones 45
Frosty chocolate bananas 44
Fruited lamb curry 75
Fruity orange baskets 62
German wine cup 33
Glacé fruits 43
Gourmet's egg flip 34
Grapefruit glory 60
Grapefruit soda pop 60
Green lasagne with beef 77
Harvest cheesecakes 27
Hawaiian pork cubes 57
Hazelnut cream gâteau 59
Herb-roasted corn cobs 26
Honeyed fruit kebabs 51
Hors d'oeuvres 34
Hot cross buns 22
Hot rum sauce 36
Iced coffee 60
Indian-style corn on the cob 53
Individual smoked salmon quiches 46
Italian baked peaches 77
Jumbo beef burgers 48
Lemon meringue basket 21
Light Christmas pudding 36
Liver sausage whip 50
Mandarin wedges 63
Marrons glacés 83
Marsala sauce 36
Mediterranean deep pizza 81
Melba sauce 51
Meringue gâteau 84
Mexicali salad 50
Mocha meringue flans 69
Mocha sauce 51
Mushroom and ham quiche 32
New potato and green pea salad 32
Orange angel frosting 18
Orange gingerbread fingers 69
Orange marvel 60
Original turkey stuffings 35
Oven-baked rice 57
Paella 73
Pancake batter 64
Party pasta with mussels 76
Pasta shells with bolognese sauce 78
Peanut dip 56
Peppermint twist 60
Perfection pork with celery 71
Petits fours 42

Pippin salad 47
Pizza dough 80
Pizzas with mozzarella 86
Plum cake with rum syrup 41
Poached salmon trout in aspic 54
Port wine jelly 35
Prawn and bacon flans 69
Puff pastry twists 16
Quick tuna curry 58
Rice and pepper salad 32
Roast turkey with festival stuffing and
  garnish 26
Rolled pineapple sandwiches 62
Sandwich loaf 86
Sangria 73
Sardine diamonds 30
Sausage and apple pielets 44
Sausage and bean soup 87
Sausage and cheese pancakes 65
Sausages with barbecue sauce 53
Savoury pancakes 66
Scalloped eggs 56
Simnel cake 24
Smothered peaches 46
Snow frosted ham 35
Spanish rice and sausage salad 73
Spiced chicken drumsticks 44
Spreads for savoury biscuits 34
Spring daisy cake 18
Spring fruit salad 33
Strawberry cream flans 54
Sweet and sour sausages 52
Sweetheart gâteau 82
Sweet pancakes 66
Swiss roll with mincemeat cream 43
Tangy prawn dip 16
Toasted coconut squares 51
Tray pizza 81
Tuna tetrazzini 77
Turkey and artichoke savoury 79
Turkey and noodle casserole 78
Uncooked tomato chutney 50
Wedding cake (2 tier) 29
White bread 86
Winter vegetable minestra 87